IN LOVING COLOUR
A Father's Perspective on Life

Timothy Ray Phillips

Twaanévie Publishing House
Blacksburg, Virginia

Daniel Books, an imprint of Twaanévie Publishing House
845 Deercroft Drive
Blacksburg, Virginia 24060
www.twaaneviepublishinghouse.com

Book Layout © 2013 BookDesignTemplates.com

Cover photo of chalk sidewalk © Christin Lola/Shutterstock. All rights reserved.

Scripture quotations marked (NIV) are taken from THE HOLY BIBLE, NEW INTERNATIONAL VERSION®, NIV® Copyright © 1973, 1978, 1984, 2011 by Biblica, Inc.® Used by permission. All rights reserved worldwide. Scripture quotations marked (NLT) are taken from the Holy Bible, New Living Translation, copyright © 1996, 2004, 2007 by Tyndale House Foundation. Used by permission of Tyndale House Publishers, Inc., Carol Stream, Illinois 60188. All rights reserved. Scripture quotations marked (Message) are taken from The Message. Copyright © 1993, 1994, 1995, 1996, 2000, 2001, 2002. Used by permission of NavPress Publishing Group.

"In a Blink" is from *The Ark of Lumijnfroost* © 2012 Timothy Ray Phillips, published by Twaanévie Publishing House. Used by permission.

Ordering Information:
Additional copies may be ordered at Amazon.com.

Queries and/or Quantity Purchase Discounts:
Contact the Publisher at twaaneviepublishinghouse@gmail.com.

In Loving Colour/ Timothy Ray Phillips. -- 1st ed.
ISBN 978-0-9660055-5-4
Library of Congress Control Number: 2015910381

Printed in the United States of America

Also by Timothy Ray Phillips

The Ark of Lumijnfroost:
A Menagerie of Verse

To my beloved trinity:

Patrick Stuart Timothy
Hannah Margaret Leslie
Andrew William Matthew

Divine Imperative

Therefore, as God's chosen people, holy and dearly loved, clothe yourselves with compassion, kindness, humility, gentleness and patience. Bear with each other and forgive whatever grievances you may have against one another. Forgive as the Lord forgave you. And over all these virtues put on love, which binds them all together in perfect unity.

Let the peace of Christ rule in your hearts, since as members of one body you were called to peace. And be thankful. Let the word of Christ dwell in you richly as you teach and admonish one another with all wisdom, and as you sing psalms, hymns and spiritual songs with gratitude in your hearts to God. And whatever you do, whether in word or deed, do it all in the name of the Lord Jesus, giving thanks to God the Father through him.

(Colossians 3:12-17 NIV)

TIMOTHY RAY PHILLIPS

A Father's Imperative

We live in a fallen world; the days of earthly paradise have passed. Our inheritance is not in this world, but in the next. So what does God expect of each of us? Do we shrug our shoulders and let the world get darker still? Or, has God called us to be a light to the world?

We are complicated creatures with an unknown but finite number of days to live in this world. We enter it naked, unknowing, and unable to walk or speak. In the span of God's blink, we will leave it and move on. Some naked and broken; others unable to move or speak. And in that blink of time, we will have done some things—good and bad—and wish we had done others. We will have built our character, the starting point for our entry into Heaven, where life is truly an eternity.

Though life seems short at times, in other ways it is long, and our memories carry some wisdom in them. I am prematurely grey, and I would like to think I owe that to an early accumulation of wisdom. Whether true or not, as a parent, it is my most important duty that I prepare you, my children, for your own journey in the storm. Life is not easy, and much of it you must do alone.

Consider these pages as you begin your journey. Refer to them from time to time. Remember, while you must do some things on your own, you are never really alone. God has marked you as eternally His, and you have your Mother and me cheering you on and encouraging you every step of the way.

Though life is short, enjoy it. Make the most of it. And, if you can add pages to this book to help your own children, I would be honoured. Make this part of your legacy, and theirs.

Finally, remember to take baby steps until you have your balance. God is patient. Enjoy the run, and don't overlook the sights along the way. Be sure to stop and catch your breath when the world is flying by too fast.

It is ok to sit and rest from time to time. The pause will give you time to think and ponder the meaning of it all. If you can, dip your pen in your creative ink and write a few chapters of your own. It will be fun to look back in your closing days and see how far you have come.

Remember in all of this that you are much loved.

In a Blink

Life happens in a blink,
pivots of a living being
lasting not even a second.
Quiet, visible heartbeats—
more than four hundred
and thirty-five million
between suckle and ashes.
Yet we blink in fear
that life will pass us by.
So we live like grasshoppers
consuming the summer green.
Yes, a few play like crickets,
but they hide in the shadows—
heard but never quite seen.
Even the beauty of the butterfly
fades in the afternoon sun,
as its paper wings fan slowly
until its short month is done.
Then, in a blink it is gone.

−TIMOTHY RAY PHILLIPS
The Ark of Lumijnfroost (2012)

TIMOTHY RAY PHILLIPS

CONTENTS

A COLOURFUL LIFE 1

OPENING THE BOX 5

1   BLACK: "INSIDE THE BOX" 7

2   WHITE: "BEGINNINGS" 9

3   GREY: "PERSPECTIVE" 13

4   SKY BLUE: "VISIONS & GOALS" 17

5   BRICK RED: "FOUNDATIONS" 21

6   ORANGE: "UNIQUENESS" 27

7   CRIMSON: "EDUCATION" 31

8   SALMON: "TENDERNESS" 35

9   PINK PIG: "IMAGINATION" 39

10   BLUE: "LOYALTY" 43

11   PERIWINKLE: "FRIENDSHIP" 47

12   PINK CARNATION: "FIRST LOVE" 51

13   IVORY: "PURITY" 55

14   CARIBBEAN GREEN: "MUSIC & LAUGHTER" ...59

15   TAN: "HEALTH" 63

16   BURNT SIENNA: "HARD CHOICES" 67

17   BLUE GREEN: "SELF-SACRIFICE" 71

18   YELLOW: "HAPPINESS" 75

19   SEA GREEN: "ADVENTURE" 81

20   MAHOGANY: "CHARACTER" 85

21   BROWN: "HARD WORK" 89

22 JUNGLE GREEN: "COMPETITION" 93

23 GREEN: "ENVY" 97

24 AQUAMARINE: "RESOLUTION" 101

25 BITTERSWEET: "DISAPPOINTMENT"..........107

26 BURNT ORANGE: "LOSS" 111

27 PURPLE HEART: "COURAGE" 117

28 INDIGO: "PRAYER" 121

29 GOLDENROD: "FAITH" 125

30 SEPIA: "MEMORIES"......................................131

31 MAROON: "REFLECTION" 135

32 VIOLET: "PASSION" 139

33 FOREST GREEN: "STEWARDSHIP"..............143

34 MIDNIGHT BLUE: "SOLITUDE" 147

35 COPPER: "TITHING".......................................149

36 MAGENTA: "POETRY" 153

37 SILVER: "RESPECT" 157

38 CORNFLOWER: "KINDNESS"..........................161

39 LAVENDER: "COMPASSION"...........................169

40 PLUM: "GENEROSITY"....................................173

41 TEAL: "HONOUR" 179

42 RED: "FORGIVENESS" 183

43 SCARLET: "GOD'S LOVE" 187

44 EBONY: "GRACE" 191

45 CANARY: "HOPE" 195

46 TURQUOISE BLUE: "PEACE" 199

47 WISTERIA: "NOSTALGIA" 205

48 GOLD: "HEAVEN" 209

IMPERATIVES & ATTRIBUTES OF THE SOUL 213

ABOUT THE AUTHOR 215

IN LOVING COLOUR
A Father's Perspective on Life

A Colourful Life

Chemically, and clinically speaking, the human body is a composition of eighteen elements of the Periodic Table. Not surprising, we are mostly hot air—65% of our constitution. Followed, at 18%, by carbon (good old Ticonderoga #2); hydrogen (10%); Nitrogen (3%); Calcium (1.5%); and, Phosphorus (1.2%). Smaller amounts include potassium, sulphur, chlorine, sodium, magnesium, iron, cobalt, copper, zinc, iodine, selenium, and fluorine. For some politicians, we might add a little helium.

It's hard sometimes to think of ourselves as just a mixture of earthly elements, but there you are.

The Bible, though, says that God made us from the clay of the earth. It should be no surprise, then, that eight of the ten most common elements found in dirt are in the chemist's preceding list. We are mostly dirt and by the time we finish life here on Earth, we will be carrying it in our pores, our hair, our lungs and even under our nails.

Yet, while our human bodies are vessels of clay, our human beings—our soul and spirit—are made altogether differently. In life, it is important that you make a clear distinction between the body and the being. One is temporary and the other eternal. The chemical composition of our bodies will break down over time, much as a giant redwood falls to the Earth and eventually becomes part of the soil again. It is a law of science, readily observed.

But our beings are of an eternal compound that cannot decompose, and that is a true gift of God. Why do I mention bodies and beings, chemicals and dirt? Science and God?

If we are to live full, rich lives on Earth, as I believe our Father in Heaven desires us to do, then we must hold a perspective that is focused not on the here-and-now, but on the eternal horizon. We all have physical aches and pains, and emotional bruises and scars. We are limited in our thinking, and perhaps more limited in our patience. If we are not careful, we will dwell on the physical structure of our bodies and on the goals of an earth-bound soul.

Dispense with the Periodic Table of the mortal man, and live a rich life that is God-inspired, Christ-desired, and Spirit-fired.

Compare the two periodic tables that follow and ask yourself which one is three-dimensional?

Elements of the Human Soul (Eternal)

Wht	Red	Brn	Orn	Yel	Gry	Grn	Blu	Pur	Blk
WHITE Beginnings	CarnPink 1st Love	Mhgny Character	ORANGE Uniqueness	Gldnrod Faith	Grey Perspective	CaribGrn MusicLaugh	AquaMrn Resolution	Lavender Compassion	BLACK Inside
Ivory Purity	PinkPig Imagination	Copper Tithing	BrntOrng Loss	Canary Hope	Silver Respect	SeaGrn Adventure	Teal Honor	Plum Generosity	Ebony Grace
	Salmon Tenderness	BrntSien Choices		Gold Heaven		GREEN Envy	TurqBlu Peace	Magenta Poetry	
	Btrswt Disappoint.	BROWN Work		YELLOW Happiness		JungleGrn Competition	SkyBlu Visions	Wisteria Dreams	
	RED Forgiveness	Sepia Memories				ForestGrn Stewardship	Periwnkl Friendship	Violet Passion	
	BrickRd Foundations	Tan Health				BluGrn SelfSacrifice	BLUE Loyalty	PrplHeart Courage	
	Crimson Education	Maroon Reflection					Cornflower Kindness	Indigo Prayer	
	Scarlet God's Love						MdntBlu Solitude		

Elements of the Human Body (Temporal)

	1	2	3	4	5	6	7	8	9	10	11	12	13	14	15	16	17	18
1	H Hydrogen 10%																	
2														C Carbon 18%	N Nitrogen 3%	O Oxygen 65%	F Fluorine <1%	
3	Na Sodium 1%	Mg Magnesium .5%												P Phosphorus 1.2%	S Sulfur 2%	Cl Chlorine .2%		
4	K Potassium 2%	Ca Calcium 1.5%						Fe Iron <.5%	Co Cobalt <.5%		Cu Copper <.5%	Zn Zinc <.5%				Se Selenium <.1%		
5																I Iodine <.5%		
6																		
7																		

Period

TIMOTHY RAY PHILLIPS

Opening the Box

Nothing says *Childhood* like a box of crayons. Flip the lid and there stand the rows of different colours, with their points not yet flattened and their wrappers still intact. Shortly after comes the familiar smell of the coloured sticks, a scent that lingers with you throughout your life, just as the memories of childhood stay with you.

Childhood is a special time in our lives when we learn to draw, when we first discover that there are choices to be made—choices we must make. It is also the time we learn there are consequences to those choices we have made.

Oops, we have made the sun green and the grass blue. What do we do? If we are a very young child, we may cry. Hopefully, if we are older, we will take a deep breath and find a way to make it better.

In childhood games there are 'do-overs.' On the big things, adulthood is not so kind. Mis-steps are not so easily undone. Yet, for people of hope, there is the God of the Universe who Himself made the colours out of nothing. To Him who made us, we are forever children and do-overs are a continual favour.

Yet we must grow as we age. Contained in this book are literary crayons, shades of our Life here on Earth, each focused on a different aspect of our life. Like a real crayon box, this book does not contain all possible colours. There is simply not enough room. But the ones included within this paper box are important areas to consider as you mature and make decisions.

Take heart in one thing, though. You, my children, have already made the most significant, life-changing decision you will ever make. You have chosen to be followers of Jesus Christ, Believers in His resurrection and promise of eternal salvation. For this, your Mother and I are eternally grateful to our Father in Heaven.

Like all mortals, your Papa is a flawed creature, but I have tried to give you my best advice on the pages that follow. Use them as you find them helpful but always let God be your true, best guide as you travel this adventurous road called Life.

I love you all and wish the five of us could travel Life's road together all the way through, but I am wise enough to know that it is not possible. But like the Holy Spirit, your Mother and I are in your hearts and were since the moment you were born.

1 BLACK:

"Inside the Box"

Inside the crayon box the colours line up neatly in rows like the good soldiers they are. Their wrappers are clean, and their heads sharp. They have not yet seen the light of day. They have not yet found a young child's grasp.

They are untested, as you were before you were born. Within each stick there are pictures and crooked letters waiting to be let loose on the page. Images not yet even imagined. Much as it was when we first learned you were a growing being, when we first heard your heart beat and saw your little limbs move on the ultrasound.

In the beginning there was darkness, a black void. *Darkness was over the surface of the deep, and the Spirit of God was hovering over the waters (Genesis 1:2 NIV)*. And there you were in the safe, warm water of your mother's womb.

Psalm 139 is my favourite of all psalms because it tells how God is there with each of us in the very beginning. He knit us in the womb and gave us our soul—that which has the potential to live for all eternity in His presence.

Remember, though, that first there is darkness, and then light. The dark always comes first. It is in the dark where we begin to grow, and our minds are dark before we begin to learn. Most important, our soul spirit are dark before our heart is open to His Spirit. Before then, there is no light hidden under the bushel. No spark at all; just a dark soul waiting to be set on fire for the Lord.

As you travel on this colourful path we call Life, remember that you started out in darkness. Then you accepted Christ as your Saviour and from that moment on, His light has been on you, and in you.

In Life there are emotions—ups and downs—and experiences at every step. Never be fooled that a Christian life is an easy one. You are guaranteed to be blessed, but you will also be tested—not so that you will fail, but that you will become stronger and more able to serve the Lord.

It is a colourful Life the Lord has given you. Enjoy each and every part of it.

You watched me as I
was being formed in utter seclusion,
as I was woven together in the dark of the womb
(Psalm 139:15 NLT).

2 WHITE:

"Beginnings"

Life starts with a clean slate, a white piece of paper. From there, we leave our mark—good or bad—for others to see.

It is impossible to know the future. Even children born with a silver spoon in their mouth have surprises along the way. Bad things that go bump in the night.

Museums and history books are full of pictures of happy families taken in the years before the Holocaust. None of them sitting in the photographer's parlour on those sun-filled days held even an inkling of the horrors to come. Had they, they would have taken the first ship across the Atlantic. Or, perhaps, banded together to stop the nightmare from taking hold.

Life is full of surprises—challenges and opportunities alike. An optimist would view the two the same. It is all a matter of perspective. In this, it is key to know that God created you and that there are things He wants you to do while you are still here on Earth.

Disappointment will cast a shadow over you from time to time much like the dark clouds rising over the hills. Whether you brave it head-on or under the rim of an umbrella, you must charge through it. Recognize the loss; let the emotion surface. Most importantly, learn from the experience.

Be the best you can be. Notice, I did not say, 'be perfect.' There is only one man in the world who was perfect, and He died for all of us so that we could live in eternity with Him and our Father in Heaven.

God does not want perfection from you, or from any of us. He does want us to live according to His Word. There is much in the Bible to guide us, but remember these two greatest commandments from the Lord:

1. *Love the Lord your God with all your heart and with all your soul and with all your mind and all your strength (Mark 12:30 NIV).*
2. *Love your neighbour as yourself (Mark 12:31 NIV).* Or, to put it another way, *in everything, do to others what you would have them do to you (Matthew 7:12 NIV).*

I firmly believe that if everyone on this Earth lived by those two principles alone, we would not have all of the problems—the wars, brutality, hatred, poverty, and such— that we have today.

We are, sadly, in a fallen world and that makes it all the more difficult to live according to those two golden principles. Sin runs deeply in all of us; it is constantly pulling us to put ourselves first and foremost.

Yet this does not mean we should not try. No, we must in many ways start over again each time we fail. And, most likely, we will fail right up to the last breath we take. But God knows what is in our heart; he sees the effort, the desire to do *Good*. He can see the Spirit from the flesh.

So stuff the crayons in your pockets and take the first steps into the bigger world. Draw life on your canvass. Try the different colours. Make a mark.

Make a difference.

Don't be afraid of mistakes. God erases what is not pleasing to Him.

As you colour, though, colour with love. It's really the only way to go.

You saw me before I was born.
Every day of my life was recorded in your book.
Every moment was laid out
before a single day had passed
(Psalm 139:16 NLT).

TIMOTHY RAY PHILLIPS

3 GREY:

"Perspective"

Very little in life is purely black or white. Life is too complicated to reside in one shade or another. Instead, life is found in the in-between, without the edge or defined border.

It is the grey matter that matters. Use your mind, God-given to you, to solve the problems of the day and to plan for the future. Mistakes will happen. The lessons learned will help you lessen future problems.

We cling to the notion that things are either black or white in order to see life simply. It is a way to cope with a complex world perhaps. So we put our lives into neat boxes, and our choices into columns—Yes/No, Left/Right, Now/Later, Right/Wrong, Red State/Blue State, Pro-Choice/Pro-Life, Believer/Non-Believer.

The irony in all this is that the more we put our life-view into boxes, the more we cramp ourselves into a box of our own. We begin to limit ourselves and learn to think only inside that box. We become content, complacent even, to live within four firm walls and gradually, like the frog in boiling water, to lose all perspective. It is how walls get built. The more time we spend inside the box, the less we see the complex world around us.

And, the world outside is complex. Make no mistake about that. Throughout your life you will be faced with choices and difficult decisions to make. This is truer for you than even your Mother and me, though we are only thirty years older than you.

Life is moving at such an incredible speed.

But how do you see beyond the black and white? How do you live and thrive within the grey? Or, better yet, move beyond the grey into the vibrant colours that are all around us? It is these colours that make life fulfilling and best prepare us for the glories of God's kingdom.

First, you must know yourself and be well-grounded. Feed yourself on God's Word. Open your heart to Christ and give yourself totally to God. He will give you His spirit and from that time on you will never face life alone.

Second, put your trust in God and learn from what He tells you. In time, that little voice inside you—call it instinct or conscience or God's whisper—will gain your attention. You will learn to feel the difference in your life when you heed this voice. Over time, your ability to hear this voice inside you will get stronger and stronger—even on a crowded dance floor. This whisper is the incorruptible Holy Spirit working on the spirit within you.

Third, keep the blinders off and your shoes untied. See the world from the other's perspective. There is generally logic in their view. Try to understand it and build from there. Do not pre-judge. That is not to say that all choices are righteous, or acceptable in God's eyes. But, remember, not everyone has travelled the same road as you. For some, the journey has been hard and seemingly unfair. It can colour their judgment and their actions can colour yours. Be careful in that. If Life were simple, it wouldn't be a life.

He who pursues righteousness and love
finds life, prosperity, and honour
(Proverbs 21:21 NIV)

TIMOTHY RAY PHILLIPS

4 Sky Blue:
"Visions & Goals"

"What do you want to be when you grow up?"

That is one of the first questions a kindergartener hears. As parents, we never stop wondering—and worrying a bit late at night—what you will one day become.

We think naturally of professions, your occupation. Our culture tends to put people into boxes, as we have learned. Will you be a cartographer or an architect? Or, perhaps a pizza delivery man. Patrick wasn't sure. Hannah has a logical, scientific mind. Would she want to be an accountant like her Papa? Andrew wanted at first to be a dentist. Then he changed his mind and considered being an entertainer. What these two professions have in common, I have no idea. But, somewhere in his own grey matter, he made the transition and made it very smoothly. One day, a dentist; the next, a comedian. Both want to make the world smile, and that's not a bad thing to make as your life's passion. In his middle teenage years he transitioned to wanting to teach high school English; then to being a pastor.

Life, though, is much more than a job and what we do from nine to five or during the graveyard shift. It is the means we have to get things done, to make a difference around us so that the world is truly a better place for us having arrived.

What is your vision? How will you have the greatest impact in the family? In the family of Believers? In the family of People?

Your impact will be greatly determined by how you approach life itself. If you view it from within the four walls of a box, you will be little noticed. Remember, also, that not all boxes have four walls. There are many ways to find yourself lost in a maze.

Think big. Really big. The sky is endless and, trite or not, so are the opportunities. Just as your life started with a blank sheet of paper, so did your limitations. You will define them as you go along, from the time you set your first goal.

It all starts with a first step. Do you begin with a hop, a skip, or a jump? Or do you stand there frozen to death, afraid to even make a move?

President Roosevelt once said that "there is nothing to fear, but fear itself." A simple statement with powerful insight. We often fail for fear of even trying. We worry too much what others will think when, truly, the only one who matters is God.

Think of blue skies. Kids, the sky's the limit. Truly, you can do anything if it is what you really want. Remember, though, that much in life is not simple. It is not enough to wish something to happen. You have to make it happen, and that usually always requires prayer, planning, persistence, perspiration, and patience. And a lot of practice. But throw in some play along the way. It will make your life more enjoyable and you more bearable to be around.

$$\text{Vision} + 7P = \text{Fulfilment of a Dream}$$

$$\text{Where, } 7P =$$

$$\text{Prayer}^3 + \text{Planning} + \text{Practice} + \text{Persistence}$$
$$+\text{Perspiration} + \text{Patience} + \text{Play}$$

Do not wear yourself out to get rich;
have the wisdom to show restraint
(Proverbs 23:4 NIV).

TIMOTHY RAY PHILLIPS

5 BRICK RED:
"Foundations"

"It may seem strange to talk about vision and then foundation. Should it not be the other way around?

If we imagine life to be a house, it makes sense to picture the height, shape, and character of the house first. That will tell you the depth and outline of the foundation that is needed to support it.

The same is true with real life. Find your passion. Set your vision to it. Then equip yourself so that you can arrive at the sweet spot that is the centre of your passion.

Equip yourself well. Be like the tree that sets down firm roots before it grows too tall. Measure and pace yourself. Know your limitations. Exceed your expectations.

Know first of all that you are a child of God and, like your Mother and I, He wants for you to succeed and to be happy. Success is in the passion. It is in the doing, not the arrival.

The foundation of your life rests on your faith in God and on His Word. The Bible is filled with real life examples of Good living, that which is pleasing to God. These are just a few:

- Noah, who laboured for 120 years building the ark while his friends and neighbours laughed at his foolishness. Who in his right mind would build such a massive boat in the middle of dry land? But Noah had heard God's voice and followed his instructions to the letter. And God rewarded Noah's faithfulness by saving him and his family from certain death in the flood. While the Earth lay underwater, Noah stood on the firm foundation of the ark, a craft designed by God.

- Moses, who gave up the comforts of Egyptian royalty to lead God's people out of slavery and toward the Promised Land.

- Ruth, who as a young widow, remained loyal to her mother-in-law Naomi. She left her homeland and people to travel with Naomi to Bethlehem. There, poor and despised as a foreigner, she worked hard in the fields to gather food for her and Naomi. She was a woman of integrity. *Your people will be my people, and your God will be my God (Ruth 1:16 NIV).*

- Daniel, who had the courage to pray to God despite the threat of death. He took his faith with him into the lion's den. While all others believed he was doomed, Daniel knew otherwise. He remained grounded in prayer. God honoured Daniel's courage and steadfast faith and brought him to safety. He elevated Daniel in the king's palace, but Daniel was wise enough to give all the glory to God.

- Paul, who recognized more than anyone that he was truly mortal and subject to temptation and sin. He fought the good fight to the end, never backing away from his past mistakes, but striving always to remain true to the teachings of his Saviour Jesus. He suffered much throughout his life, but he persevered— not only for his salvation but for everyone he ever met. He was never ashamed to place his candle—his faith in Jesus—in plain view for all to see.

- David, who was a man after God's own heart. He was the youngest of eight sons, a shepherd boy, and yet he was the one whom God chose to be the greatest king of Israel. He stood up to the giant Goliath and slayed him. He wrote songs and poems honouring God.

- Jonathan, who was a loyal friend to David. He knew that God is the ultimate source of truth, and he based his choices on that knowledge. Throughout his life he was conflicted by the evil desires of his father, King Saul, and the loyalty he felt for his friend David. He had a keen heart that could hear the desires of God, and those desires favoured David. Often, today, you will face the conflicting choice of the modern world and God's truth. There will be anguishing moments at times. Be like Jonathan; have courage and be loyal to God and His truth.

- Jacob, who once wrestled with God by the River Jordan in order to earn His blessing. Although it did not happen all at once, he came to realize how much he depended on God for his survival and future.

Setting a solid foundation, you will learn soon enough, is the important task in preparing for life and in supporting the life. It is also the least understood and appreciated.

When we open a board game, most of us are so anxious to start to play we forget to read the directions. We therefore don't fully appreciate the intricacies of the game—the best strategy for winning, having fun, and avoiding the pitfalls all at the same time. For many, the joy is in the doing, not the planning. Yet part-way through confusion sets in. They reach a crossroads and have no idea how to proceed.

If you consider that each of our lives is such a game, and a unique one at that, you will realize that it has never been played before. We cannot trust our own instincts because we are not the creator of the game. But there is one who does know. We must trust His words when He says we must build our foundation on rock. We must rely totally on Him.

Kids are anxious to grow up and live in the world. By age ten, you know everything and are ready to drive a car and head out of town. Trust me: by thirty you will begin to look in the rear-view mirror and by forty you will dream about being a kid again. Swinging in a tire or riding your bike on the country roads will be the things you most want to do. You will long to return to the adventures of the afternoon when you explored in the woods and dirtied your hands near the underground springs.

The world is a tough, dangerous place. Your only way to survive and succeed is to prepare. Build a foundation that best supports your eternal perspective.

Noah may have built the great ark, but it was God who supplied the blueprint and the list of materials. He even prepared the list of passengers.

Moses, the great leader, may have led his people out of slavery and toward the Promised Land, but it was God who led and fed the thousands upon thousands of people. Moses gave the law, the Ten Commandments, to the Israelites, but it was God who created them and carved them into stone.

If your foundation is not Christ-centred, you will never survive to the other side. Now, when you are young, is the time to prepare, and prepare well.

The rain came down, the streams rose,
and the winds blew and beat against that house;
yet it did not fall,
because it had its foundation on the rock
(Matthew 7:25 NIV).

TIMOTHY RAY PHILLIPS

6 ORANGE:

"Uniqueness"

The Bible says that we are created in God's image. Yet we are each made to be individuals. There is no one else in the world with the identical DNA as you. Even identical twins have slight deviations, and the traumas and experiences of life itself cause different changes in their physical appearance. My father is an identical twin, and yet he is a good three inches shorter than his brother.

Besides the physical, there is the more important soul— our true inner being. It is our seat, our personality. The essence of who we are. Our thoughts and feelings and ability to make decisions. And, yes, our free will—that very same will that got us into trouble in the Garden of Eden.

We are all born with a soul, that blank sheet of paper. Our free will is like the artist's pen. We draw as we speak, as we walk, as we do, as we feel, as we choose.

As you can imagine, there are infinite ways a soul can grow. Even those born in the same house soon become unique, one of a kind. An individual child of God. All seven billion souls now living. And all those between Adam and Eve and ourselves.

There is little you can do to avoid being unique. It is inescapable. Even those growing up in a commune are distinct from each other. Teenagers try to look and act and speak alike, but they are, in the end, unique.

One of the keys to life is to celebrate your uniqueness. Relish it. Embrace it. Enjoy it. You are a masterpiece in God's eyes, and in your Mother's and mine.

Consider these words as you approach adolescence and adulthood:

We each develop physically, emotionally, and spiritually at a pace unique to ourselves and known only by God. Your body, for example, may begin adolescence before or after your friends. Not to worry. Eventually, by the time you are out of high school, you will physically be the adult you were meant to be. This may be small comfort to you if you are either an early or late bloomer, but keep this in mind because it is true.

With respect to our bodies, we were not created equal. Learn to be comfortable with the size, shape, and features that make you, you. Let good health, not your appearance, be the main motivation in seeking a better body.

We mature emotionally independent of our age. I have seen five-year-olds who behave more grown-up than twenty-five-year-olds. Do not be too anxious to grow up before your time. By the same token, childhood must eventually be put behind you. At some point, the caterpillar has to leave the safety of the trees and find his wings as a butterfly.

In terms of your spirituality, we are forever children before God. Unlike our bodies which peak before we are twenty, our spirits have the capacity to grow daily. An open heart is essential, followed by an open and inquiring mind. Listen to the whispers. They will tell you more than all the shouts combined.

The world at large seems concerned most with physical beauty, followed by emotional/mental health, and, last, some sort of 'spiritual bent.' This is completely backwards. Focus on your spiritual health. Be right with God, and emotional and mortal health will naturally follow.

Finally, always be grateful to God that He created you in His image and instilled in you a soul, unique in itself, and a treasure-trove of gifts. Serve the Lord in your own unique way.

The sun has one kind of splendour,
the moon another and the stars another;
and star differs from star in splendour
(1 Corinthians 15:41 NIV).

TIMOTHY RAY PHILLIPS

7 CRIMSON:
"Education"

We learn from everything we do. From formal lessons in the classroom to our experiences in the real world. Education is a life-long endeavour.

The challenge for children and young adults is to embrace education as a fun, worthwhile experience. Take reading, for example. You can view it as a chore to read so many pages each night, or as a unique opportunity to escape in the shoes of someone different or to travel to a different place or time or realm.

In work, my most important criteria when I evaluate people is their ability to learn from their mistakes (or even those of their colleagues). Do they apply the lessons learned? Do they even notice when a mistake has been made? Can they pin-point the cause and find the best solution? How well can they adapt to change?

These are important questions on a planet that spins a thousand miles an hour. We live in the Information Age, and more information is being created every second than the poor human brain can possibly compile and digest, let alone use at a later date.

Education is all about preparing for the present and the future. It is about learning to connect the dots, much like those animal pictures on a child's menu. Only, in real life, the pictures get a lot more complicated and the answers are not always so obvious. And, oh yeah, there's usually time pressure involved.

Competition in the world is fierce. That is the way God made us. Look at Cain and Abel. A mighty tough world, especially for poor Abel. God put a creative spark and a driving force in each of us. He hopes that both will be used to seek Him, but He also gave us free will. Man, being man, we strive for things that are beyond the original scope.

Work is rarely fun. If it was, they wouldn't call it work. But ever since the fall of Man, we have been commanded to work. It is a punishment designed to make us stronger and more prepared for Heaven. Education—active learning—is how we best equip ourselves for this challenge.

For kids, 'homework' is a double four-letter word. It's a struggle to get them to open the books and do the problems. But the reality is, without the practice, there is little chance of success on the test—in the real world. Try telling that to an eight-year-old and all you get is a rolling of the eyes and a half-collapsing walk as they feign desperation.

Practice makes perfect. We hear that often, and it's true. With each effort, we do it faster and with less errors. Study and practice are the initial foundations of a solid education, followed quickly by actual experience. We learn best by doing. That is why summer jobs and internships are so important. In the process you learn how to do, but also what you like and dislike. Better to find out the summer before your sophomore year of college than the summer after graduation.

Education comes through hard choices. Do you do your homework or go outside and play? Go to school or play hooky? Are you engaged in class or merely skating by? Do you learn as much from your failures as your successes? Many would argue that the opportunity for learning is greater in failure than success. The former has a way of forcing a person to question everything. It is part of that driving force inside us that seeks perfection, that seeks the impossible.

Never be ashamed to learn. Never pretend to know it all. Step up to the plate and ask for guidance. Demand a solid education. It is your best ticket to a fruitful life.

By wisdom a house is built,
and through understanding it is established;
through knowledge its rooms are filled
with rare and beautiful treasures
(Proverbs 24:3 NIV).

8 SALMON:

"Tenderness"

Experts in mental health will tell you that an early sign of a troubled youth is his mistreatment of animals. Watch out for the boys who pull off the wings of flies. Watch them carefully.

On the other hand, marvel at the boy who is mesmerized by a woolly caterpillar crawling along his finger. Or who cries at the sight of a dried butterfly on the side of the road.

You can judge a lot about people, about their character, by how they treat those who are weaker than they. Historians certainly say that about a nation.

Our society today has made some strides. It is now normal, expected even, for a father to be emotionally and physically involved in raising his children. I have changed many a diaper and, though not the most pleasant of things, it does somehow strengthen the invisible bond between a parent and child. You see your child at his or her most dependent state. Just as much as when you feed them or carry them in a papoose on your chest where they fall asleep listening to your beating heart. It is the closest feeling a father will have to carrying a child in the womb. You feel every little kick and movement, every stretch and yawn.

The thought reminds me of the night before Patrick was born. The doctors were concerned with his pending delivery so they attached a heart monitor to him while he was still in the womb. His Mom and I fell asleep in the dark room listening to his heartbeat. A loud, healthy heartbeat. In many ways, it seemed as if I were still in my mother's womb, and my life had not yet begun.

It was a safe night—my last one. Once you are a parent, you never sleep well again. You can't; there isn't enough tenderness in the world and so you spend your time worrying about everything that could go wrong.

I believe if there is one great disappointment God has in us, it is our inability to be tender in all things and with all people. We are often downright mean. It is a terrible habit we picked up from Cain and even the great flood in Noah's time didn't purge it from our common character.

It takes a strong person to take the first step and be kind to a stranger or, even worse, a perceived enemy. It takes an even stronger boy or man to show tenderness in his dealings with others. We assume tenderness is not masculine and that is it a sign of weakness. But we know Jesus was tender, and He is God. How much stronger could He be than that!

We live in a fallen world; we know that. Perfection awaits us in Heaven. Until then, we must do the best we can. God expects no less from us. He expects us to take care of those who need our help. He expects us to walk in peace and love, to admire the beauty—His creation—that surrounds us. He expects us not to fight and if struck, to turn the other cheek. Contrary to belief, turning the other cheek takes far more courage than striking the person with your fist.

I wish there were more poets and writers and artists in the world. I wish there was more quiet than noise. More tenderness than violence. More sharing than poverty. More than anything, I wish we all had never outgrown the tenderness we had had as a new-born child.

Let your gentleness be evident to all.
The Lord is near
(Philippians 4:5 NIV).

TIMOTHY RAY PHILLIPS

9 PINK PIG:
"Imagination"

We are all children at heart. In some ways, many ways, we become more childlike the older we get. At times during the day I want to sneak home and crawl into bed and return to my childhood dreams of cowboys and steam trains.

I want to go exploring in the Pennsylvania woods again and play in the stream and the underground springs near our home. I want to fly kites and roller-skate when I should instead be at work.

We were created in God's image. Just as there is the Holy Trinity (Father, Son, and Holy Spirit), humans are a triune creature. God created us out of the earth, giving us our physical body. He added to the mix His breath of life. In that very instant we received both our soul—with its ability to think, imagine, feel, and initiate—and our spirit, with its innate connection to God. Body, Soul, Spirit. The human triune.

We are the only creatures on Earth to contain all three. A pink pig may have a soul—that is, a mind, a strong will, emotions, a perky personality, and the ability to relate to other pigs and other animals, including man. But he doesn't have a spirit that connects to God.

When God formed us out of the earth, we were more like a fertile rain forest than the dry Sahara. God gave us a playful imagination knowing we would use it. In our soul is the ancient memory of the Garden of Eden. There is a nudging inside us, a genetic need to be playful and creative. We are not robots. Nor are we ninety-eight year-old school marms.

The familiar, pleasing smell of Play-Doh is a powerful scent. I would venture that the hands of every chief executive officer in America, as well as the President, once felt the cool dough between his or her fingers. Give a yellow or blue canister to one and see if it isn't opened within a minute.

We were made in God's image and therefore born to create. Our hands yearn to play with clay and finger-paints and good old-fashioned mud. Our toes wiggle in a rainstorm in high hopes of jumping in puddles again. We breathe against the cold windows and draw with our fingers in the foggy pane. We write "Wash Me" on every dirty car we see. We want to lick the frosting bowl and snitch the cookie dough when our wives or moms aren't looking.

We are imaginative animals with a playful soul. We dream in colour even when our eyes are wide open. We can picture the Man in the Moon, and see the clouds as ships crossing the blue sky. We put ourselves on those very ships and look back at the Earth beneath miles of ocean sky. We can imagine animals talking and men flying.

We have a sense of humour and can laugh at ourselves when life seems just a bit too serious. Yet we all know people who see the cup half-empty and their life half over. They have forgotten what it is to play and think of "what if's." They walk around the rain puddles and see a leaf on the water as it is, not what it could be. They have let the Play-Doh dry up and their marbles get lost.

Imagine how peaceful the world would be if every gun was replaced with a crayon. All in a single nano-second. Quick, draw! What if everyone climbed a tree once a week and played hopscotch with their kids before supper?

Don't be in such a hurry to grow up and be like us. It is the adults who need to grow down and be more like you. It is inevitable that your bodies will mature, but your soul has the ability to stay young and playful.

Let your imagination run wild in the halls of your mind. Think young. Be playful outside the box. Be like Hannah and give a voice to a favourite stuffed animal; relish the possibilities.

And the next time you think about walking around a puddle, stop. Grin, and then jump as high as you can to make the biggest splash possible. You'll put a smile on God's face, as well as your own.

Tonight my son says he will be a buffalo in his sleep. He asks me what animal I will be in my own dream tonight. I answer a 'firefly,' but he says that is a thing too small for a dream. What about a bear? No, they don't get along with buffalo. Finally, I know the answer. A giraffe. I've always wanted to be tall.

He looks at me with a big smile and nods. OK, a giraffe it is. Tomorrow, I'll be a little grey rabbit with a wicked personality.

The mountains turned playful
and skipped like rams,
the hills frolicked like spring lambs
(Psalm 114:4, Message).

10 BLUE:
"Loyalty"

True blue. A high mark indeed.

In thinking about loyalty, it is important not to leave out the first step—discernment. It is a word that is not often used these days. It means to be able to look at something and know, really understand, its core essence. If you discern someone's motives, for example, it means that you consider the situation from that person's perspective—from all angles. You look at the situation critically, and that doesn't mean negatively but, rather, you see it thoroughly and objectively.

You must always discern first what is in a person's heart, what is in their nature. Then, and only then, do you consider which side you will support. Having decided—and decided well—that's when you are to remain steadfast in your support.

Loyalty to a cause or a friend in whom you believe is admirable and, I believe, pleasing to God. Loyalty unde-served is, at best, misguided; at worst, it could be tragic. It is heroic and admirable to go down with the ship, to fight until your last breath if such a cause is worthy of your efforts. In that, God will reward you.

If you haven't discovered it yet, on the playground or in the classroom, the strong and the mean can sense the weak and the meek. When a lion chases a herd of zebra, he doesn't try to catch them all. He only needs one to have his feast.

And what do the brave zebra do? Nature has taught them to scatter. While some would argue there is strength in numbers, the flip argument says to disperse—each man for himself—knowing that it is not possible for one lion to slay forty zebra. For thirty-nine of the zebra, the odds are in their favour. But pity the poor one. He has just had his last savannah meal.

Where are his friends? What if one day they tried something different, and they all circled around the lion, stood on their hind two legs and trampled him into a lion-skin rug? Surely, one (by now, bewildered and befuddled) lion would be no match for a whole herd.

In any situation, what changes the tide? What invisible force takes hold and emboldens the masses to believe that they can make a difference, that the particular cause is worth the risk? The once mighty Iron Curtain held back the human spirit in the East of Europe for forty years. Then in an almost breath-taking pace, countries behind the Iron Curtain were liberated with hardly a shot fired. The Berlin Wall came down and no officials or their armies on the eastern side could change the tide.

At some point in their history, loyalties changed. People began to discern what was true and right. The more they discerned and understood, the more courage they found within themselves. All that was waiting was a catalyst, someone to push the snowball down the hill.

Loyalty is highly prized in our world. Often, it is crafted in a way that forces you to choose sides. It is the leader's way to test your commitment to them and their cause. In this way, loyalty is very much tied to the subject of hard choices.

In life you will find yourself constantly at a cross-road where you must make a choice. Do you continue on the original course (i.e., remain loyal to the current endeavour) or do you re-evaluate and re-direct your efforts? Again, blind loyalty is not a virtue. Neither is fickleness. So it should be obvious that the best solution is to evaluate something thoroughly before you commit.

I mention the word *fickle.* It is important. Doubtless in your life you will find yourself in a leadership role when your troops begin to waver. This generally happens when the situation at hand is getting tougher and the risks higher. In these situations we are the most tempted. Anyone can be a pilgrim at the start of a journey. It takes true passion and commitment to finish the job.

Don't be surprised or disappointed if you find yourself alone beneath dark clouds of a gathering storm. First, with God on your side you are never really alone, and He will see you through to the end. Second, He will never give you more than you can handle. Never. And that is something you can take with you to your eternal home in Heaven.

You can prepare yourself, though, by knowing your teammates as best you can. Measure the strength of their spirit; gauge their integrity; and, observe how they treat others. Perhaps most important, understand how they have

handled themselves in prior storms. Be prepared and remember that in any storm God is your umbrella.

A friend is always loyal,
and a brother is born to help in time of need
(Proverbs 17:17 NLT).

11 PERIWINKLE:
"Friendship"

Good friends can make a great childhood. Lousy ones can be disastrous. I know this from first-hand experience. When I was ten, my family moved from Northern California to Pennsylvania. Moving at any age is tough but it is particularly difficult going into adolescence. In the late sixties, before the cell phone, internet, and cable television, there was a huge cultural difference between California and the East Coast, particularly in conservative Lancaster County, PA.

Needless to say, my transition was not a smooth one. I was short, my voice was on the high side, and for the life of me, I could not keep my R's straight from my W's. Everyone wanted to know why I talked so funny. In some ways, they assumed I had a California accent, which only made me feel more different than the rest of them who seemed to have known each other since the day they were born.

On top of all that, I have always been fairly shy until I get to really know someone well. For a new kid at school, this was instantly translated as being a snob. Coming from California only exacerbated the effect. Finally, I was a straight arrow, a goody-two-shoes.

I was relatively sheltered at home, either because I was the "baby" in the family and/or because being the introspective type, it suited my personality. Either way, it meant that by the time we moved and I was approaching a brand new school and a new set of kids, I was totally unprepared socially. For me, the next eight years were long and lonely ones. The worst years of my life actually.

That is not to say I didn't have friends. I did. The problem was they were not very good ones. They suffered much in the loyalty department. I can still recall, somewhat painfully even now, being nominated by one of my friends for a class position. All of the candidates were sent out to the hallway while the class voted. We walked back in a few minutes later and to my embarrassment and hurt, I alone had received not a single vote. Not even the person who nominated me dared vote for me.

I was devastated, and I know it only lowered my confidence—in myself and in my friends. The moment still haunts me in middle life. It is interesting how much sway our childhood has over us well into adulthood. I think from that time on I was more cautious (if that was possible) in sharing of myself and making myself vulnerable—two components vitally important to developing healthy friendships.

In all honesty, I have been a cautious friend all my life. I have seen friends come and go over the years. Now, my best, true friend is your Mother. In her, I have the full confidence that she has my best interests truly at heart. With her, I can share any thought or feeling. This is truly a great blessing to any marriage.

However, I also believe that every man should have a good friend, a loyal friend, of the same sex. A man needs another man to talk with, relate to, and hang around with. Maybe it's a carryover from childhood. Even though a person is grown up, sometimes you still want to go outside and play ball until the yard is well into darkness.

The same is true for women, though I believe they have an easier time developing friendships than men do, especially in adulthood. It is hard to get men to open up. Maybe I'm not the only one who had a lonely childhood after all.

I share my story with you to help you understand that it is important to have friends throughout your life. Your ability to develop healthy friendships will greatly improve your journey to maturity and a healthy self-esteem.

Friendships require a certain degree of give-and-take to be truly genuine, healthy, and long-lasting. If you ever feel it is one-sided (even if it is to your benefit), you should take a step back and re-evaluate the relationship. A true friendship is based on mutual respect, common values, and similar interests.

Choose your friends wisely and be sure you have each other's best interests at heart. Be as true to your friends as Jonathan was to King David. Choose someone who will watch your back, not work against you behind your back.

Choose someone whose values are similar to your own. As you are already learning, this is a tough world, full of sin and perils. The purpose of your journey here is to prepare your soul for eternity in Heaven. By design, God will place many people along your path. Some will be helpful; others will not. Some will need your help; others will not want it.

You can survive on your own, most likely, but it will not be as rewarding as it would be if you were with a group of friends. As I said, middle school and high school were extremely lonely times for me (and I pray they will not be for you), but I learned a lesson in that and I broke out of my shell when I entered college. Trust me, there is no greater feeling than being part of a group that treats you as one of their own. Whether that be your Christian family, your birth family, or your family of friends.

Friendship is a gift from God. Like all such gifts, be glad and enjoy it fully. The Bible says that *a person standing alone can be attacked and defeated, but two can stand back-to-back and conquer. Three are even better, for a triple-braided cord is not easily broken (Ecclesiastes 4:12 NLT)*. This advice, from King Solomon, arguably the wisest man who ever lived.

He also writes that *wounds from a friend can be trusted and are better than many kisses from an enemy (Proverbs 27:6 NLT)*. True friends will tell you what you need to hear; they will hold you accountable for living a righteous life. But they will have your best interests at heart. Enemies, on the other hand, will tell you what they know you want to hear. The purpose of their words will suit their interests, not yours.

As iron sharpens iron,
a friend sharpens a friend
(Proverbs 27:17 NLT).

12 PINK CARNATION:
"First Love"

You will always remember your first love. Rarely will the two of you marry. It is first a fact of life, the law of probability. I believe God paired us up even before our birth. The likelihood that each of us would find that person right off is far remote.

Nor do I think that you are ready for that person early on. We grow and change with each experience, good and bad. I am convinced that if your Mom and I had met each other when we were sixteen, we never would have married. I had too much growing up yet to do. I needed to see the world first. Literally.

So what does all this mean? To you? The power of first love is incredible, immense. It will send the innards of your brain bouncing off its walls. It will race your heart like a twelve story elevator drop. It will make you feel more special than at any time before.

It will make you do crazy things, and put wild notions in your head. And in all this, it will even take your breath away.

Odds are, before hand, it will feel to you that everyone around you, everyone but you, is now in love for the first time. This will only build the pressure and anticipation.

"When, Lord, when?" "Why me, Lord; why must I wait?" "How long will I wait?"

If you are like me, in your teen years, you will feel like an Israelite wandering forty years in the desert in search of the Promised Land. The Israelites were not a patient people at that time. Time can move painfully slow when you are anxious for a change, especially a change that is brand new to you.

It is a long journey from first grade Valentine's Day parties with pink and red paper hearts graced with cupids and cartoon characters. A long time since construction paper mail boxes on the back of your classroom chair. A very long time since you held your first box of conversation hearts and giggled at "Kiss Me" and "Cutie Pie."

You move into Middle School and find yourself at your first dance. You are standing on the fringe holding up the wall and watching everyone else dance. You drink a lot of sherbet punch and can feel every drop of hot sweat slide slowly down the inside of your cold arms.

As always in these situations, time is moving much too slowly. You feel like the night will never end. You half hope to be on the dance floor right then, and half dread it. Even the girl you get along so well with in class can seem like a deaf-mute in a slow dance. The dancing is so stiff and, yet, you long for it and long to get through it and past it. It is a rite of passage, and you just want to get it in the memory book and come out unscathed on the other side.

There's a reason they call your first love a crush. By the time it is over, whether it has lasted a day or a year, your heart will feel torn because of it. First loves are all bittersweet because the emotions and the expectations are set so high. We don't know what to expect going in, but we want it to feel great. We want to be placed on top of the world for the rest of our days. We are anxious to live the life of a grown-up.

But, like all things mortal, the air escapes from the balloon and we come back to Earth. It is gravity doing its job. Whether we land on our feet in a better place depends on our attitude and our resilience. Both of these flow from our character, our emotional foundation.

Simply put, they reflect the depth of our self-esteem. Do we believe in ourselves? Do we recognize that we are a good person and that sometimes the chemistry just isn't there?

Chemistry between two people is a magical science. Like all things science, it must be approached with respect, and you must keep a clear head, watch for signs of trouble, and be prepared for the possibility of an explosion!

Love is an explosive emotion that is best handled with care. Remember, though, this important thing in all things human: what is old hat for the rest of us is a new experience for you. Enjoy that experience; be excited that you are in love. But keep a cool head while your heart is warming, and rush into nothing. If it is meant to be, God has already made the ultimate arrangement of time and place. Listen to your heart, and keep your heart open to the counsel of others, including and especially God's.

TIMOTHY RAY PHILLIPS

Be happy, young man, while you are young,
and let your heart give you joy
in the days of your youth
(Ecclesiastes 11:9 NIV).

13 IVORY:
"Purity"

When we were in Canada several years ago, we stood on the Athabasca Glacier. It was on Canada Day, in the middle of the year, and yet it was biting cold. A serious avalanche had occurred overlooking that spot just three weeks earlier.

The amazing part of that trip was that while we stood there, beneath our feet, the glacier was slowly melting over time. A small creek of ice-cold water ran through its middle. We were able to cup our hands and drink water that had most recently fallen as snow a hundred and fifty years ago.

Our guide pointed out something that we took for granted. The air quality in 1850 was far purer then than it is today. The water we were now drinking was the purest natural water to ever touch our lips. As I shoved my now red, swollen hands into my jacket pockets, I looked around at the ivory expanse and thought about his comment.

Purity, like clean air and water, is taken for granted by most of us. Quality standards shift gradually, much like the pace of a retreating glacier. A postcard-width a year. So gradual, in fact, that you rarely notice the change. We tend to compare today's quality to yesterday's and, often, the change is nearly imperceptible. Yet if we could compare it to Day 1, we would probably be shocked at the level of degradation.

This is true with the environment (air, water, open space, toxins in the home and work) and also with the moral fibre of our nation. Standards do change over the years. Sometimes, the change is for society's betterment. Other times, though, the loosening is more the reflection of laziness and lack of respect than it is a measure of maturity.

Until the 1960s, men routinely wore hats in public. In the 21st Century I have seen men wear shorts and sandals to weddings, as well as funerals. Some might call it individuality; I call it lack of respect.

This is all probably a natural course of events. Any scientist will tell you that heat dissipates over time. Scholars of the Bible believe that the gene pool of Man in early times was much purer than it is today, which could help explain their longevity. Noah, for example, lived to be over nine hundred years. In all honesty, I'm not sure I could take that much of my fellow man.

Nowadays, cancer of all types is becoming more and more common. Either because of environmental factors and/or a deterioration of the gene pool.

Purity can be measured to many things, but is closely tied to one's character and, for that matter, the character of one's village or nation. Do the actual contents inside you mirror the appearance on the outside? That is a key question to ask yourself throughout your life.

Here are a few things to consider:

1. Purity is defined as *a* freedom *from adulteration, contamination, or immorality.* Focus on the word <u>freedom</u>. Most people see *purity* as a constraint, a chore, or limitation (of fun, in particular). But it is actually keeping you free of the consequences of an impure life.

2. Purity is not the same as perfection. We are called to live a pure life with Christ as our example. But our nature is sinful from the get-go; it is in the DNA of our soul. There is only one perfect person who ever walked this Earth, and He is our Saviour. Don't use perfection as an excuse to not strive for purity.

3. Removing impurities is a lot more work than preventing them from entering your life in the first place. Just ask British Petroleum who spent over forty billion dollars to clean the Gulf after the massive Deepwater Horizon oil spill leaked 210 million gallons of oil into the sea.

4. Impurities tend to disperse and impact a wider area. Those millions of gallons of leaked oil were pulled and carried by the ocean currents, affecting all of the Gulf-Coast States, hundreds of miles of beaches, and thousands and thousands of marine life. Oil once contained miles below the sea bed now rests on the sea floor, with unknown impacts on marine life and the food chain.

5. Impurities bring unknown consequences. It is only years later that those consequences surface and, by then, the damage has been done.
6. Impurities mask the true quality. Add a drop of yellow dye to glass with blue-coloured water and it changes to green. The blue colour is lost forever; it has so blended with the yellow that is cannot separated.
7. Most important, though, when something is pure, you receive the full benefit of that purity.

Once you have tasted glacial water, it is hard to go back to the tap. Let the experiences of a pure, Christ-centred life fill you with spiritual joy. And let that joy in your spirit be the driver in your life here on Earth.

Don't let anyone look down on you
because you are young,
but set an example for the believers
in speech, in life,
in love, in faith, and in purity
(1 Timothy 4:12 NIV).

14 CARIBBEAN GREEN:
"Music & Laughter"

Laughter is music to the ears, yours and God's. We were created with a sense of humour. I like to call it our seventh sense—God's perfect number. Intuitively, we know that it is far better, far healthier, to go through life happy, not sad; optimistic, not pessimistic; giving, not holding back.

You have, I know, heard the expression that it takes more muscles to frown than to smile. Physically, it is more work to scowl, but yet we fall easily into the Downer's Trap. Don't you do it.

Laugh to your heart's content. One secret is to not take yourself, or life, too seriously. It's ok to laugh at yourself when you do something silly. Look for the funny side of things. Let your funny bone have a little fun. Lean on it from time to time.

I am prone to giggle fits and when they hit me, afterwards, I can feel the tensions of life go away. It is such a good feeling to be rid of the pressure and angst of a modern life.

As the Scripture says in Ecclesiastes, there is a time to be sad and to cry, but there is definitely a time to laugh. You know already, even in your short lives, that the Earth is a tough, rough place to live. Fallen Man has seen to that. But in every desert there is an oasis, a Caribbean paradise, where cool refreshment thrives, where life triumphs over death.

You, as a Believer, can be a walking oasis, a bright spot against the backdrop of a serious life. Unlike an oasis that is stationary, you are able to move through life touching people in good and humorous ways.

Make music wherever you go. Let it be your music, though, wholly original and reflecting your own style. Be like the man who carries a harmonica in his pocket so he can make music wherever he rests.

I remember in my college days walking through the shady streets of small Blacksburg, Virginia and hearing a boy play the blues on his harmonica. I had to stop and listen. It was one of those moments that stay with you the rest of your life. You know in the instant you are living it that you are in one of those special moments. It creates a unique feeling that you immediately file in your memory.

Your memory is your life. Millions of moments stacked together like a flip-o-rama. When you flip through them all, you see your life re-animated.

Do you like what you see then? What you hear? Is there much music or laughter?

These two, music and laughter, have much in common, you know. I have yet to meet a person who hums or sings during the day who is not also happy. I know for me that when I am happy, content with my life, I find it hard not to hum. There is a connection between a happy heart and playful spirit.

Why go through life in a serious state or a sad one? Or a quiet one, for that matter? Sure, there are times when you relish the peace and quiet, when you want to stop and think things through. Meditation is good for the spirit and the soul. Meditation surely beats medication in that way. But don't think too long and hard. God didn't make life that complicated; man did.

I believe God would be content to see us as simple shepherds or farmers who worked hard in the day, made music in the evening, and wrote poetry at night before bed. He would be content to see us as fishermen who gave thanks to Him before and after each catch. He would be happy to see us work and live side by side in peace. That is life. To be born and grow up in His shadow; to be good and faithful stewards; to grow towards Him; and, to pass over the threshold from mortal life to eternity with Him. Pure and simple.

It is man who dams the rivers and builds the cities. Who creates the machines and places materiality above all else. It is man who enjoys complexity and strives to clone the mystery of life. It is not enough to marvel at life; man must analyse it to death.

Don't complicate your life with complexity. Learn a thing or two from the Amish. Keep it simple, and stay true to your focus on God and what He wants for you. Enjoy the people around you. Make full use of your gifts He has given you.

Make music, whether it be with an instrument or your own imagination. Most important, laugh out loud a lot. Don't worry too much about life. If you stay in God's shadow, He will watch over you. As a father, I can tell you there is no greater sound that that of giggling ones playing in the near distance.

Cry when you must; Smile when you can; Laugh in between.

A time to cry and a time to laugh.
A time to grieve and a time to dance
(Ecclesiastes 3:4 NLT).

15 TAN:
"Health"

When I was growing up in the 70's getting a suntan was all the rage. My brother even went out and bought a sun-lamp. All of us spent time in front of it. We were trying to make up for the Pennsylvania weather.

Of course, years later, we learned about skin cancer and the harmful rays of the sun. Now, I slap on Sunblock 86 whenever I'm going to be out in the sun for more than fif-teen minutes. Oh, and of course, I wear the big Amish hat to boot. Better safe than sorry.

Then there're the 14,000 different diets out there, each claiming to give you a long fulfilled life. The reality is that all we need is moderation in all things.

Here, then, is my recipe for a healthy life. Follow this closely, and enjoy the difference:

1. Sleep like a baby eight hours every day.
2. Drink like a camel. At least a hump a day.
3. Eat like a rabbit. Fresh fruit and vegetables.

4. Whistle like a parakeet when you work.
5. Laugh like a hyena at least twice a day.
6. Run around like a monkey sometime between your whistle and your laugh.
7. Relax with the buffalo before dinner.
8. Swim with the dolphins.
9. Stretch beyond the giraffe's reach.
10. Soar like an eagle over the Grand Canyon.

Good health involves the mind, body, and spirit. If any of them are ill, you will suffer. Maintaining good health for all three involves daily exercise and learning to read the signs when the health is declining.

Exercise your mind every day. Challenge yourself to think through problems, to find creative solutions. Think outside the box. Never accept the accepted unless you are satisfied that it makes sense. Build on lessons learned. Create new things with your mind. Imagine the impossible, and then do it. Write a poem—and forget the rhyme.

Exercise your body every day. Stretch. Elevate your heartbeat at least twenty minutes. Build a good sweat. Find a competitive sport and have fun. Avoid drugs and smoking. Avoid anything that will harm your body. Remain sexually pure.

Read the Bible every day. Struggle with the hard truths inscribed in God's Word. Challenge yourself to hear the spirit within you. Let the Holy Spirit speak to you in new ways. Apply what you learn to your daily living. Be a true Christian. Live out the Word, and make a difference in the World. Be a light for God's Word.

Let Christ be the cornerstone of your life here on Earth. What better way to prepare for an eternity with Him in Heaven.

> *Heal me, O Lord, and I will be healed;*
> *save me and I will be saved,*
> *for you are the one I praise*
> *(Jeremiah 17:14 NIV).*

16 BURNT SIENNA:
"Hard Choices"

The crux of this matter lies with our free will. God could easily have chosen to make us robotic good deed do-ers who never had a negative thought in the brain or so much as squished a baby ant.

He could have made us all in the likeness of Jesus Himself. There would be no need for anyone to wear *What Would Jesus Do* bracelets; we would act like Jesus automatically, whether by divine promotion or a nudging of our own conscience. God would be universally beloved. The world would be one in spirit from the beginning to the eternal end.

For you, wouldn't it be great to have everyone in the world like you and consider you to be their best friend? Wouldn't it be great to know that everyone you ever met would always be on your side? No more worrying about dark alleys or wondering why someone was being nice to you.

What if we could know for certain that every decision we made, every move, was motivated by the purest of interests? What if we could know that every decision we ever made would always be the right one?

- Should I take French or German? Or Latin?
- Should I go out on a date with this person?
- Should I trust her?
- Should I try smoking?
- Should I go to a party that could get wild?
- Should I listen to my "friends" or my conscience?
- Should I honour a commitment or go to the beach?
- Should I go to college?
- Should I buy a car or save for a house?
- Should I follow my long-term dreams or take the easy road?
- Should I stand up for what is right or remain silent?
- Should I accept responsibility for my actions or make excuses?

Part of the thrill of life is knowing that anything can happen. Even the best made plans can go awry. What joy is there in making choices if there is no risk? The reward comes in knowing we had to make a sacrifice. If Disneyland was free, at some point it would become a ghost town of sorts. At the very least, we would take it for granted. Its value, its specialness, would be gone in short order.

Life, as you have already discovered, is not at all risk-free. You can take nothing for granted. Every decision, by its nature, involves making a choice, and that choice involves making a sacrifice. You cannot be in two places at one time. You cannot diminish your health and preserve it at the same time. You must choose. You cannot study and go to a party at the same time. You cannot want a healthy lifestyle and then take up smoking or drinking. You cannot save money and squander money simultaneously.

Life is all about making hard choices. It is also about making mistakes and hopefully learning quickly from them. We call that maturity. Sometimes, it will seem as neither option is a good one, and you are forced to choose the lesser of two evils. That is part of life. You have to deal with it. At other times, it will seem as if you can't lose no matter which way you go. You might be right sometimes, but more often than not, there is a flaw in your logic, and the sure-fire bet is not that at all.

Be careful when you are on the threshold of a decision that you are looking at it from all sides. Look beyond the short-term gain and good feeling to see the true cost. Approach your decisions with an eternal perspective. Whenever possible, sleep on it for a day or two. Pray often and listen to God's spirit that is within you.

Finally, know always that it is inevitable that you will make poor choices. Know even more that, despite those choices, your Mother and I will continue to love you and hold you in high regard. And that is even more true for your Father in Heaven.

Commit to the Lord whatever you do,
and your plans will succeed
(Proverbs 16:3 NIV).

TIMOTHY RAY PHILLIPS

17 BLUE GREEN:

"Self-Sacrifice"

When I think of self-sacrifice, Mother Theresa immediately comes to mind. She was a modern-day saint who gave totally to society's weakest and most unadmired. She was wholly committed to serving others.

We can't all be like Mother Theresa...or can we?

Life is simple. It is also complicated. Even the simplest design can be a maze when you replicate it six billion times or more, each a heart-strand next to the other. Throw in the emotions of mortality, and you have a volatile world.

Sometimes the answers to life's questions are amazingly simple. Only we assume anything at all related to life must also be complicated. It is like on a school exam and you finish ten minutes before all the others. You are at first relieved. Then, as you sit and quietly look around, you start doubting yourself. You begin to worry that maybe you misread the questions; maybe it was filled with trick questions and you blew through it too quickly. Maybe you blew the test completely.

Why do we do that to ourselves? Why do we lose our nerve as soon as we have figured out a life's lesson? Why do we lack the confidence?

The answer there, too, is quite simple. We put our confidence in the wrong place. We put our trust in ourselves, in our ability to solve the problem rather than relying on God. Our Self wants to control everything in our lives but somehow, in the back of our mind, where our spirit lives, we know better.

The same is true with our priorities. We tend to put our own interests ahead of others, sometimes even our own family. Half of all marriages end in divorce, and the reasons given are varied. But they are only excuses of our selfish Souls. The real reason for all divorce is a lack of self-sacrifice.

Sacrifice is a word Americans are not used to hearing. It has been generations, World War II to be precise, since Americans have really had to sacrifice in a significant way. Emotionally, we have lost touch with the word. We have been living in the "Me" generation for the past forty-plus years.

This inability to put others' interests before our own is a key factor in the strange society we have today. It is why marriages break up so easily. It is why people end friendships so quickly. It is why people switch jobs every two or three years when they start getting bored and feel "unfulfilled." It is why we have become an impatient nation that wants quick fixes, solutions that require little effort from us. The shock of 9-11 jolted us back to the centre but in just a few short years our self-centred focus has again become the norm.

As long as our focus remains inward, we will fail to grow in a meaningful way. The solution is with us, but the answer is not. That is, as Believers, we have the Holy Spirit dwelling within us, and it is the Spirit that will lead us to Him. The answer, though, to Life's great mystery is not contained in our soul; it resides in Heaven.

We were made for God's pleasure, not the other way around. I know it is a shock to discover we are the Earth and God is the Sun. We revolve around Him, and He provides us light and the strength to grow.

When you were little, you were always asking questions. Now that you are older, it is time to start asking the same question: Why. Why are you doing something? Who does it serve? Others are yourself?

If you are serving others, you are serving God, and your focus is proper. If you are helping only yourself, your motives are not pure, and you need to reconsider.

When we serve others, we serve God. We bring others into the light, and that is an honourable thing to do. God will bless you for this, both today and in Heaven.

As I have previously written, be generous of your time and talent and treasure. Seek out the underdog and give him a much needed hand. Consider others first. I know it is a difficult thing to do sometimes, but you must.

Although the mortal side of us wants to be selfish, the eternal side knows better. Let your spirit reign over your soul and lead you a step closer to God.

Set a good example in this, and you will see a powerful difference in your life along the way. Besides blessing yourself and others, you will come to know true happiness firsthand and up-close.

Remember one last thing in all you do: To God be the glory.

Do nothing out of selfish ambition or vain conceit,
but in humility consider others better than yourselves.
Each of you should look not only to your own interests,
but also to the interests of others
(Philippians 2:3 NIV).

18 YELLOW:
"Happiness"

What makes you happy?

Seems like a good, logical question. It's a tough one to answer, though. Clearly, everyone in the world wants to be happy. I have never yet met a person who prefers misery over happiness. Yet we know fair well that much of the world today is full of angst.

I personally do not think it is a matter of knowing what it takes and being unable to attain it. Rather, I believe most people honestly do not know what leads to happiness.

When you are a child, it is more straight-forward:

$$Happiness = Toys + Playtime + Milk \& Cookies$$

A little older, and the desire for money and power and prestige enters into the mix. As do girlfriends and boyfriends and the strong need to feel all grown up. As you approach middle-age and the greater likelihood of pending death, the issue of leaving behind a legacy looms front and centre.

This is all common and, therefore, predictable. So because we know this and still aren't happy, there must be a different, more valuable approach to this question.

Let's start at the beginning—the moment before God put the breath of life into Adam and animated the dust. Did God intend for Adam to be happy? Was the first man created with the intention that he would be happy throughout his life?

We know that shortly after Adam's birth, God said that it was not good for man to be alone. By "good," did He not mean 'happy?' God knew that He had designed a social creature. It would be impossible for Adam to have lived alone forever and, remember, before his Fall, Adam was expected to live forever in the Garden of Eden. The garden contained the Tree of Life, and God made no commands against Adam eating its fruit.

To ensure Adam's happiness, God created Eve from Adam's rib. Now there were two social butterflies living in complete innocence (happiness) in an Earthly paradise where food was plentiful—at arm's reach—and their protection secured. In fact, they were so blissful, they probably never gave a second thought to fear. They had no knowledge of evil at that point in their lives.

They were free to play all day if they so chose. The very idea of work—toiling for their own food—was not introduced until they had committed the great sin and fell from God's grace. They were kicked out of the garden into a hard life of pain and difficult work. Later, they would experience the intense emotional heartache of losing one child at the hands of another.

Is this meant to imply or suggest that happiness comes
from an idle day of play and pampering? Of course, not.
Some of the richest people on Earth are the most unhappy.
Some of the poorest are the happiest.

I believe the mystery lies deeper in the Garden. There,
Adam and Eve communicated directly and daily with their
Creator. The Bible tells us, in fact, that God walked among
them in the coolness of the Garden (Genesis 3:8). He con-
versed with them as well. What utter joy it would be for
us to now walk side by side with our Lord. To stand physically at His side and to hear His voice.

Before the Fall of Man, before Adam and Eve committed
their first sin and disobeyed God's direct command, the two
humans were spiritually connected to God in a unique and
intensely personal way. Their spirits were on the same
wavelength as God and, just as importantly, their spirits
had control over both their soul (their mortal ego) and
body. There was a balance of order that kept the white
noise of life from interfering with their relationship (communion) with God.

The sin against God that fateful day changed all of that.
Adam and Eve put their own desires over God's, even
though God's commandment was given to protect Adam
and Eve from the very sin they committed. That is, He
knew, as only God could, that the Knowledge of Good and
Evil would feed their egos and pride and fool the two into
believing they no longer needed God. Even though He had
created them out of nothing and had placed them in paradise.

That, my children, is the power and danger of man's
ego. Whenever we convince ourselves that we can go it

alone without God's help, we set us up for an eventual fall that is every bit as deadly as Adam and Eve's.

So I have discovered the elusive answer to happiness.

Happiness comes from a total dependence on God. Mind you, I said 'total,' not 'partial' or 'half-hearted' or 'when it fits my lifestyle or busy calendar.'

Our conflict with our life is that since the Fall, our spirit inside has never regained the position it once had over our soul and our body. As a result, we feel, on a nagging sub-conscious level, that our relationship with our Heavenly Father, the one who created us, is not as it was meant to be. As long as our spirit is out of joy, we can never be truly happy—not on the course of our life.

We can enjoy a massive chocolate sundae and feel like we're in Heaven, but the happiness is gone within the hour. So much for bodily pleasures. I note strongly here that the same is true with drugs, though worse. In time, more and more of the drug will be required to reach the same effect. But always, it is short-lived. Remember that if you are ever tempted down that road. It truly is a dead-end path. Put this in your mind before you are yet tempted and keep it in the forefront so that, unlike Eve, you will be able to resist the temptation.

What about the soul? Can it be happy long-term? Your soul looks at life through its (that is, your) perspective, not God's. It wants to constantly steer the ship of You, even though God set the stars in the sky and is the great navigator.

Your soul assumes happiness comes when your ego is stoked. Every time you get an A on a test, win a school election, go on a date with a pretty girl or handsome boy, graduate from college, win a game, publish a book.

But have you ever noticed that the joy from each of these is very short-lived. You will be happy about your "A" on a test only as long as you continue to get "A's." As soon as you get anything less, that initial happiness—the happiness you assumed would last forever—will disappear quicker than last allowance.

Any accomplishment that puts yourself ahead of others at the expense of God will never bring long-lasting happiness. It is a mortal happiness and has no chance of lasting.

If not the body, and not the soul, there is only one possibility left, and that is the spirit. When you put your talents and efforts to the glory of God, you strengthen the spirit inside you. It comes from looking at life from an eternal perspective, not a mortal one. Whereas your soul is your human personality, your spirit is your true, inner self, the part of you that is your connection to God.

God intends for you to be happy, to be blessed. His ultimate intention, from the very beginning, before Adam first opened his eyes, was that we would be in complete and perfect communion with Him at all times.

Here is a simple test that you can take whenever you feel discouraged or disappointed. Ask yourself one question: Am I feeling the loss through my soul or my spirit? Had the opposite outcome occurred, would it have glorified you or God?

When we hurt or feel like a loser, it is hard to ask that question, but it is the quickest way out of your funk because ninety-nine percent of the time, it is your soul that is wounded. You're human. It's bound to be that way. But if you want to go through life happy and with a purpose, your focus must be on the Lord, not on yourself. When you serve others, you serve the Lord and are doing His work. And, for that, you will be blessed many times over.

I know that there is nothing better for men
than to be happy and do good while they live.
That everyone may eat and drink,
and find satisfaction in all his toil—
this is the gift of God
(Ecclesiastes 3:12 NIV).

19 SEA GREEN:
"Adventure"

...is an undertaking of uncertain outcome. It is the undertaking, not the outcome. It is the doing, not the completion. It is starting something on faith, with no absolute assurance that it will end well.

Adventures need not be a trip around the world in a wooden ship. Or a dogsled to the North Pole. Or a swim among the dolphins in an ocean where sharks could be nearby.

No. It is any time you act on faith—not that you will be successful, but that God will provide and watch over you.

Life is an adventure in itself. It is a journey of faith. It is anytime you take your blinders off and step outside the box. Watch out for the Box; it will trap you all your life if it can—all the way until you are laid to rest in yet another box.

I know people who have done the same job for forty years, under the same routine each day. They wake up one morning, and they are sixty-five and all the possibilities of the past are behind them. God gave them sixty-five years to explore and enjoy His beauty, and they squandered the opportunity because they were filled with fear.

Fear is the Devil's charm. He will use it to keep you from seeing the world. He has great fear himself should God's people venture out of their boxes, their comfort zones, and have an impact on the rest of the world. He worries that we will all rise out of our desk chairs and discover the world.

Swap your desk chair, then, for a deck chair on something that moves. And when you have seen enough from the portside, pick yourself up and cross the bow to see how the starboard side lives. Never be content with the same view. Be intrigued by God's masterful nature. Don't just look at the ocean and marvel at its endless space. Dip your toe in the water. In all my travels, I make it a point to put my feet in every body of water. Even in Lake Michigan in an early spring in Chicago.

Don't just climb atop a glacier. Taste the melted ice running down its middle. It's the sweetest, purest water you will ever taste. Where else can you taste the snows from three centuries ago, when the only greenhouse gas on the planet was the flatulence of an aristocratic gardener under glass! You will feel the chill in your veins transfer to your bones and at that point, you will feel very much alive. The memory of that will last beyond the memory of summer's heat.

Remember, there can be adventure in all you do. When you walk to school, choose a different route sometimes.

Ride your bike instead of walking. Try a new sport. Attempt something you have never done before. Meet new people and make yourself be known.

When you are older, go away to college and experience life on campus. Have a midnight snowball battle with a couple hundred other students. Go camping on a small island. Hike to waterfalls and swim in the cold water. Take classes in subjects that are foreign to you. Form life-long friendships with people equally adventuresome.

Several years after college, I was transferred to work in London and Germany for a year and a half. It was in a lot of ways a terrifying time—professionally, culturally, and linguistically—and certainly emotionally. At the time I thought I had made the most of my time in Europe. It is only now, twenty years later, that I see how much I held back and kept myself from knowing the full experience. It is lost time, a missed opportunity.

Live each moment wisely and fully. Assume you will see that sight only once in your life. Often, that will be the case. Take full advantage of the moment.

Leave your burdens, your fears, and your material possessions behind you and enjoy God's world. In this way, you will be fully prepared for your journey in Heaven.

Cast your bread upon the waters,
for after many days you will find it again
(Ecclesiastes 11:1 NIV).

20 MAHOGANY:
"Character"

Your character is everything. It is the sum of your worth. It is your bond. It is the core of who you are as a human being, as a Christian. It is your moral and ethical compass. It is the ingrained principles that guide you in the important decisions that you must make.

And the not so important ones as well. A person drops a dollar bill on the street. Do you call their attention to it? It is only a dollar, though it may be that person's last. It may be the difference between whether they can take the bus to visit a dying parent or pay for a sick child's medicine. But it's only a dollar.

The little compromises do add up. They chip away at one's character, little by little until the compass is no longer reliable in setting a straight course. We perfect our conscience in the small things. Sudden sea-changes are rare; it is the little things, though, that will prepare us for the big crises that will appear on our doorstep from time to time.

And they will appear. Make no mistake about that. Life is full of surprises, and not always good ones. How will you respond? Will your character be prepared to steer you through the right choices?

I believe that your inner character is quite visible to others around you. Humans are, by nature, people-watchers. They observe constantly. When a situation occurs, they watch to see how others will react. They are looking for the leaders and the failures—and the cheaters and the phonies and the cowards. They are looking to see who is the *real deal* and who is artificial. Like Diogenes who walked the streets of Athens in the daylight with a lantern looking for an honest man, we are all on a life-long search for an honest person.

Your strong character—your honesty, integrity, fortitude, courage—can be a lantern for others. A light that can lead them out of spiritual darkness into the light of Jesus. Likewise, if you are living well, your friends, neighbours and colleagues will know you are a Christian, and they will be waiting (some hoping) for you to fall. It will validate their belief that Christianity is a religion for hypocrites; it will justify their spiritual darkness. The mind is a powerful tool, and it can justify anything; it can turn the illogical into the logical. That is one of Satan's most effective weapons.

Don't give him the chance to keep others from the light. Be true to God's Word. Be courageous in your beliefs. It is a trite, but true, bumper sticker: 'Christians aren't perfect, just forgiven.' Never put the burden of perfection on yourself. That right is reserved to one—Jesus Christ. When you make a mistake, no matter how large, take a deep breath and confess it to both God and the person you have offended.   Ask for forgiveness.   Correct the error. Learn from it, and move on.

This simple process will do more to build character than anything else I know. Admitting a mistake is a sign of being a healthy human.

Forget trying to be a superman. Being human is enough of a job.

And remember this test. If you can sleep like a baby, chances are you are well with your spirit—and your character—is intact.

Better to be lowly in spirit
and among the oppressed,
than to share in plunder with the proud
(Proverbs 16:19 NIV).

TIMOTHY RAY PHILLIPS

21 BROWN:
"Hard Work"

Hard work. Two words that strike a chord with me. Must be part of my Protestant heritage, an inheritance of sorts. My parents were lucky in one sense. The moment I got home from school the first thing I did was crack open the books and start on my homework. I would never play until my homework was done. It is part of my nature and lives in me to this day, though I have left the schoolbooks behind decades ago.

Some people believe that hard work is a punishment from God, our penitence for Adam and Eve's original sin in the Garden of Eden. In Genesis 3:19 the Bible says that God drove Adam and Eve from the Garden and that their continued survival depended on the two of them toiling for their food. They were no longer in a cool, lush garden where plump fruit hung within arm's reach.

We are made out of the brown dust, and to the dust we will return.

I take a more positive view. *I know that there is nothing better for men than to be happy and do good while they live. That everyone may eat and drink, and find satisfaction in all his toil—this is the gift of God (Ecclesiastes 3:12-13 NIV).* I do not believe that God gives bad gifts. After all, He gave us all the best gift He could—His own Son. Our very entryway into eternity.

My view is that, like any exercise, work keeps our minds, bodies, and spirits in top form. It is part of the mystery of God that He would design something that on the surface (from our perspective) has no lasting value when, in fact, it prepares us to be in the eternal presence of God. Jesus Himself commanded that we *should love the Lord [our] God with all [our] heart and with all [our] soul and with all [our] mind. This is the first and greatest commandment"* (Matthew 22:37-38 NIV).

Without work, we would be pretty pudgy people with muddled minds and no desire to follow God's heart. There would be no drive to stay in shape or improve the condition of man. Just look at those who have retired. Within short order, many have died of sheer boredom. They have lost the passion for living because they no longer see their purpose in life.

You know the expression, *Nothing in life is free,* and it's true. To each of us, God has given our share of gifts and talents, and to those who have been given much, much is expected. You have been blessed with good health, intelligence, creativity, and passion. Put these gifts to use daily, and share the fruits of your labour with those you love and those who are in need.

I leave you with a final proverb: *He who works his land will have abundant food, but the one who chases fantasies will have his fill of poverty (Proverbs 28:19 NIV).*

Remember, as long as you are a citizen of Earth, you still need to eat—and sleep. *People who work hard sleep well (Ecclesiastes 5:12 NLT).*

All hard work brings a profit,
but mere talk leads only to poverty
(Proverbs 14:23 NIV).

To enjoy your work and accept your lot in life—
that is indeed a gift from God.
People who do this rarely look with sorrow
on the past, for God has given them reasons for joy
(Ecclesiastes 5:19-20 NLT).

TIMOTHY RAY PHILLIPS

22 Jungle Green:
"Competition"

It all starts in the sandbox. There are three children and only one shovel. What's does a child do?

There are three children in a family and Papa has only two hands. What does a parent do?

You and a friend have a crush on the same girl? What does a friend do?

You are one of forty people applying for a single job. What does a hungry bread earner do?

You and a colleague are vying for the same promotion. What do you do?

God has given you a body, a soul, and a spirit. Each wants to be in charge of the others? What is a Believer to do?

Competition, healthy or otherwise, is all around us. We live on a planet of finite resources. The world's population is explosive, which places even greater demands on those limited resources. In addition, the more developed world is getting more materialistic day by day which, again, adds to the fierce competition for resources.

In the mortal world there can only be one King of the Mountain and everyone seems to want to stand on the crest and proclaim that he or she is on top of the world. That is our soul talking, not our spirit.

From an eternal perspective there is but one king, and He is the One true God of the universe. In the heavenly realm, we are all equal before Him. He who created us loves us. It is that simple. There is no need to jockey for a space in Heaven. It has been made to fit us all:

Jesus said: *In my Father's house are many rooms; if it were not so, I would have told you. I am going there to prepare a place for you (John 14:2 NIV).*

Likewise, there is no need to push our brothers and sisters aside to hold God's hand. He can hold us all in His palm at the same time. That is the nature and power of God. He is patient and will wait for the slowest one to arrive.

So here we have an interesting divide: the Heavenly realm and the mortal Earth. The Spirit and the Soul. From the spiritual perspective, as I have said, there is no competition. God is available to all of us. His grace and love are free, and it is His desire that we all believe in Him and live with Him in Heaven.

Yet we know from human history that there is competition all around us. It feeds war and envy and poverty. So if these ills are not coming from the Heavenly realm, they must reside in the mortal world. In man, to be precise. Fallen Man.

It is the pride of our soul that pushes us to have the best toys in the sandbox if not, in fact, all of them. It is our pride, our lust for earthly pleasures, that urges us to keep up with the Jones'. To have the largest and finest houses and the fastest cars and most expensive clothes. To jet set with the cream of society—or at least the most famous and photogenic. Simply put, it is our mortal pride that wants us to be the first in line, every time.

Competition is not necessarily bad. It depends on the motive and the desired outcome. If you are competing in order to do your best, that could be an admirable thing. Could be. The true test is why you want to do your best. If it furthers God's kingdom, then it is admirable. If it inflates your ego, chances are it is not healthy for your spirit's sake.

Healthy competition is all about perspective. It does not mean that you go through life with no ambition or as a milquetoast or with the word "Loser" taped to your back.

Keep your focus on God and listen to His Spirit who dwells in you. Your own spirit will discern what is right. This is where compassion comes into the picture. In every competition there are winners and there are losers, and often the stakes are stacked against the underprivileged. Many in the world are born at the bottom of a deep well with no rope or ladder and very little light.

God's grace, though, is the great equalizer. Jesus spoke of this in his Sermon on the Mount when He said that blessed are the poor and the meek. As God's Son, He knew that His Father's love is offered to anyone who asks.

Think of your life as a marathon of eighty plus years. You are running alongside only one person—Jesus. Like any smart athlete, you must let Him, the stronger of you, set the pace. Follow His lead, with all your heart and soul and mind and strength.

Keep your eyes on Him and you won't fall far from the trail. Don't worry if you stumble. He is the good runner. He will stop and pick you up.

You know from God's Word that it is a race where everyone can win. Do your best to help others find their way. Sharing the Good News is one of the best ways to shift the focus of competition from Mine to the True Vine, Our Lord and Saviour.

Stay alert, though. There will be others who show up in the race and will try to lead you along another path, but don't be distracted. They will whisper in your ear and give you false directions. Listen to His Spirit inside you.

Run barefoot if you must, but finish the race with your arms held high. Cross the finish line, the threshold of Heaven, with the full confidence of a true Believer who honoured God by helping others along the narrow way.

Similarly, if anyone competes as an athlete,
he does not receive the victor's crown
unless he competes according to the rules
(2 Timothy 2:5 NIV)

23 GREEN:
"Envy"

It begins on the playground. There are three children and only one tricycle. The little boy's chubby, sticky fingers hold tight to the handlebars. His eyes narrow; he has no thought of giving it up to the other two boys.

'Mine.' He repeats the word firmly. Over and over again, as his eyes look on the one boy and then the other. His knuckles turn white as he tightens his grip.

When the red-haired boy finally makes a move, the possessor raises his arm and declares firmly, 'Mine!' Red is prepared to fight for these wheels, while the third boy starts to cry. He prefers Mom to come outside and make the bigger boy share.

Such is life. There are defenders, fighters, and criers. Sadly, very few sharers. For most, it is all too much of a risk that the trike will not be returned, or that the other will use it to get further ahead. Or worse, that he will use the toy as a weapon. Such is life.

The world around us is green. It is the second most common colour, after the blue of the sky and sea. We are surrounded by it and, yet, we take it for granted.

Grass is everywhere and, yet, we always look beyond our own hedge and wonder what it would be like to stand in our neighbour's yard, to play in his sandbox. With all its new toys.

"The grass is always greener..." You will hear that expression an unknown number of times in your lifetime, and you will wince each time you hear it. We always want what we don't have. That is human nature, from the time of Adam and Eve and the bright pear they shared. Sometimes—perhaps often—what we want is not always what is best for us. Adam and Eve learned that the very hard way.

So have I. I have spent many years wishing for the 'perfect place' to live. When I lived in Pennsylvania, I wished I was back in California. When I lived again in California, I wished I was back in Pennsylvania. When I lived in Germany, I wished I was again in California. In London I longed to return to the States. Now, twenty-plus years later, I wish I could again live in England.

I believe God put a drop of wanderlust in each of us. We are in continual search of paradise when, in fact, we will not see paradise until we have left this Earth and returned to our one, true Father. So why the wanderlust? I have wondered about that a lot lately, and the only answer I have found so far is that God wants us to always be searching for the 'sweet spot.' He does not want us to get too content with earthly things. We must prepare ourselves for a life of eternity, and that preparation requires that we develop a character that mirrors God's.

We must lose those things that are not worthy of him. Envy is at the top of the list. It is envy that drives men to behave like men. To behave like toddlers, like childish souls who have no capacity for sharing or helping.

Be content with what God has blessed you with. Do your best in order to please God and in that, you will please yourself. There is a difference between doing your best and wanting what others have.

Be happy for those who are also blessed by God. Do not second-guess the Father who gives to each of us according to our needs.

A heart at peace gives life to the body,
but envy rots the bones.
(Proverbs 14:30 NIV)

People who live only for wealth
come to the end of their lives
as naked and empty-handed
as on the day they were born
(Ecclesiastes 5:15 NLT).

TIMOTHY RAY PHILLIPS

24 AQUAMARINE:
"Resolution"

Can truth change? Can moral truth be changed?

If stealing is wrong, is it always wrong? Can the definition of stealing be modified through the centuries, or is the
definition so clear and logical it should be left alone? Should
the definition be consistent through the ages?

If I take something that knowingly doesn't belong to me
without permission, isn't that stealing?

Resolution is the ability, the gift, to distinguish two distinct but somewhat similar objects from each other. It is
the ability to see things clearly. We first think of the resolution of a picture. Is the image clear? Can we identify the
different objects?

It is also the ability to hold fast to something, to an
ideal. Think of New Year's resolutions, where we make a
commitment to do better in school, to exercise daily, or to
watch what we eat. The implication is that we will make

a positive change in our lives and then are resolved (determined) to adhering to the change going forward.

It is a simple two-step process covered by this one important word. First, we see clearly between right and wrong. Second, we remain determined to stay on the side of what is right.

The Bible uses the word steadfast. We are to remain loyal to God's Word and His purpose. He has given us many gifts, and one of them is a conscience, the ability to discern right from wrong. He has given us resolution not only physically with our eyes but spiritually with our conscience.

The modern age has seen many Biblical virtues watered down. While God loves the different shades of colour (why wouldn't He; He created them.), there are some aspects of living that are meant to be black and white. There is light, and there is dark. Love and sin. Heaven and Hell. Right and wrong.

Today, society worries a lot about offending people. Since the original truth may be offensive to some, the rules of civil conduct are relaxed, watered down, to the lowest common denominator.

There are many obvious problems to this approach. First, is the famous "slippery slope." Anyone who has ever dieted knows that it is far harder to give up the first cookie than it is the second. And the third and fourth. Who can eat just one handful of peanuts? Once you move the line in the sand once, your resolution becomes less determined, less resolute, and you are far likelier to revise the line a second time.

This concept is true with drugs as well. Most heroin addicts did not start heroin on the first day. They worked their way toward it, and as they regressed, their resolution became more blurred, and their life spiralled down the societal drain.

As mere mortals, our systems can handle only so much temptation. If we choose to rely on our own strength, rather than God's, we should not be surprised by the adverse outcome.

As Christians, we believe that the Bible is the inspired Word of God. How presumptuous, then, for us to assume the role of editor. God wrote the script; it is ours to follow.

A second problem with changing morals is the negative effect it has on society itself. Throughout the Bible, God provides us with wise rules of engagement. If we live according to His Word, He will bless our lives. In short, the One who is all-knowing knows what is best for us.

Consider His wisdom:

- ❖ *Love your neighbour as yourself (Mark 12:31 NIV).*
- ❖ *Ask and it will be given to you; seek and you will find; knock and the door will be opened to you. For everyone who asks receives; he who seeks finds; and to him who knocks, the door will be opened (Matthew 7:7-8 NIV).*
- ❖ *Do not judge, and you will not be judged. Do not condemn, and you will not be condemned. Forgive, and you will be forgiven (Luke 6:37 NIV).*
- ❖ *No one lights a lamp and hides it in a jar or puts it under a bed. Instead he puts it on a stand, so that those who come in can see the light (Luke 8:16 NIV).*
- ❖ *'Rejoice with me; I have found my lost sheep.' I tell you that in the same way there will be more rejoicing in heaven over one sinner who repents than over*

ninety-nine righteous persons who do not need to repent (Luke 15:6-7 NIV).

❖ *Many are the plan's in a man's heart, but it is the Lord's purpose that prevails (Proverbs 19:21 NIV).*

❖ *"For I know the plans I have for you," declares the LORD, "plans to prosper you and not to harm you, plans to give you hope and a future" (Jeremiah 29:11 NIV).*

❖ *Nevertheless, the righteous will hold to their ways, and those with clean hands will grow stronger (Job 17:9 NIV).*

❖ *For the LORD watches over the way of the righteous, but the way of the wicked will perish (Psalm 1:6 NIV).*

❖ *For surely, O LORD, you bless the righteous; you surround them with your favour as with a shield (Psalm 5:12 NIV).*

❖ *O righteous God, who searches minds and hearts, bring to an end the violence of the wicked and make the righteous secure (Psalm 7:9 NIV).*

❖ *The eyes of the LORD are on the righteous and his ears are attentive to their cry (Psalm 34:15 NIV).*

❖ *The righteous cry out, and the LORD hears them; he delivers them from all their troubles (Psalm 34:17 NIV).*

❖ *He holds victory in store for the upright, he is a shield to those whose walk is blameless, for he guards the course of the just and protects the way of his faithful ones. Then you will understand what is right and just and fair—every good path. For wisdom will enter your heart, and knowledge will be pleasant to your* soul. *Discretion will protect you, and understanding will guard you (Proverbs 2: 7-11 NIV).*

❖ *Thus you will walk in the ways of good men and keep to the paths of the righteous (Proverbs 2:20 NIV).*

You will keep in perfect peace
him whose mind is steadfast,
because he trusts in you
(Isaiah 26:3 NIV).

TIMOTHY RAY PHILLIPS

25 BITTERSWEET:
"Disappointment"

Doubtless in your life you will face disappointments head on. Sometimes they will careen down the street at ninety miles an hour; other times they will strike from out of the blue. Some will devastate you to the edge of your spirit; others will just chip away and leave their mark. We are not in a perfect world; we are not yet in Paradise.

Expect disappointment. People, by nature, will put their priorities in their own order, and it may not even be a close match to yours. This is true even with best friends, and those are the disappointments that can hurt the most and do the most long-term damage to your sensibilities.

Sometimes things just weren't meant to be, whether it be a desired relationship, acceptance into college, a certain job, or the sale of a heartfelt manuscript. Some dreams are just elusive, disappointing and frustrating though that may be.

From an eternal perspective, I believe there are divine reasons for everything. God has a purpose in everything. I know from my own life's disappointments that something better has always followed. I may not have recognized it then, but later it appeared to me crystal clear.

My Grampa died in 1988 and afterwards I moved in with Ganna, your great-grandmother, so she would not be alone. The time I lived with her was such a blessing to me, and I have memories with her I otherwise would never have had.

In addition, and most important to you, I began attending church in Downey where she lived. I met a man there whose wife was a first grade teacher at Alameda Elementary. It was she who arranged for your Mother and me to meet on a blind date. Had I not moved in with Ganna, I would never have met your Mother, and the three of you would just be sparks and wishes in this Irishman's poetic heart.

You can make your life a journey of cups half-filled or half-empty. The choice is really yours. The key is to find the right balance of recognizing disappointment is a common part of life without becoming so cynical you depress those around you, including yourself.

It is trite but worth the words. When life gives you lemons, make lemonade. Every storm ends with a rainbow. If there weren't bumps and curves in the road, it would be a pretty boring journey. You might even fall asleep and miss the sights along the way.

Keep an eternal perspective in the forefront of your mind. When you find yourself getting overwhelmed by disappointment, focus on God and ask for His divine guidance and intervention. As a Believer, you carry the Holy Spirit within you, so you are never alone. And your Mother and I are in your heart as well.

"Do not be afraid or discouraged,
for the LORD is the one who goes before you.
He will be with you;
he will neither fail you nor forsake you"
(Deuteronomy 31:8 NLT).

TIMOTHY RAY PHILLIPS

26 BURNT ORANGE:

"Loss"

Scattered feathers on the ground are a tell-tale sign of a mischievous cat, and the sure-fire sign of a dead bird. But you will never see the actual bird again. The cat has seen to that.

You look at the strewn feathers, blue on white, and you can imagine the kind of bird that it was. Chances are, you heard him sing countless times in the backyard among all the others. But you couldn't pick him out of a line-up on the telephone wire. You gave him little thought until now. Because now he is gone, and you know that a life has passed from this Earth never to return again. It reminds you of your own mortality.

Now you see the grounded feathers and know that a certain life is gone. The bird will sing no more. If you are one who believes that animals join us in Heaven, then the little creature has taken his last flight home.

Loss in general is very much like this. We tend to appreciate, miss, and mourn something greater than anything we ever did while it was around us every day. In short, we often take things for granted.

There is something very human about the way we handle loss. We have the capacity to process memories, and to transfer our emotions on to them. Though we believe in eternal life, there is a real fear of the unknown, of actually crossing to the other side.

Each loss is a reminder that we ourselves are one step closer to leaving the Earth as well. And though we will leave behind the burden of our weak flesh, our souls are nonetheless nervous about the inevitable journey.

There are, of course, other losses besides death. Friends who have come into our lives and, for one reason or another, are no longer a part of it. We reminisce in our minds about the fun times and great adventures and intimate talks. We wonder why we drifted or whether circumstances will ever bring us back together. We mourn the death of a friendship, no matter how short it was.

We mourn the passing of time—our youth and innocence. Many a mid-life crisis begins with the pre-occupation with our expired youth; now older and wiser, we want to go back and re-do our younger years. We want to fix all our mistakes and un-do our embarrassing moments. We want to do it right. But, really, what is gone, is gone, and all you can lose now is the current time you are wasting trying to go back.

We mourn the loss of pets, our near friends. Dogs and cats and birds and rabbits and fish and turtles. Hamsters and guinea pigs. Mice and snakes, though hopefully not together. They were dear creatures who played in our past and kept us company. But, sadly, they grew up so fast.

We mourn the loss of values, and culture, and traditions. Men haven't worn real hats since the 50's, and not everyone dresses up for church or weddings or funerals. Any language is now permissible in public, and any lifestyle acceptable in this new relative world of ours. It is rare nowadays to find men and women of real substance and character in positions of importance.

We mourn the loss of natural beauty. Wild habitation forever changed. Houses built on beautiful hills; fields replaced with buildings or parking lots. Rivers dammed; forests cut; mountains mined. Animals driven to extinction. We mourn them because we know they can never be brought back. We mourn the loss because we know, deep in our sub-conscious that God put us in charge of them with the command that we would take care of them. We mourn because we know we have failed them, and ourselves. And, of course, God Himself.

We mourn the loss of souls. Good friends, family, and neighbours who are not moved by the light shining on the bushel, who have not been moved to accept the gift of the Holy Spirit. They remain in darkness and, for some, any attempt to bring them closer only pushes them further away. This is the greatest loss of all because once we are in Heaven, all earthly losses will fade away to nothing. There will be such reunions and resulting joy in Heaven when we arrive at last.

What, then, should you make of loss? You will never escape the sadness that comes from it. That is part of what it means to be human. If you trust in God, though, you will rely on His infinite wisdom to see you through.

God has given each of us a free will, but I also believe in the Scripture that says, *in all things God works for the good of those who love him, who have been called according to his purpose (Romans 8:28 NIV).* God has a master plan for the world's salvation that none of us can possibly understand. Our mortal minds are not equipped to see in God's divine dimension.

I want to give you a few words of advice and comfort:

1. Don't defer your love. Appreciate your family and friends today and every day. The day will come when they must leave—either physically or emotionally. Know that you made the most of the time you had together.
2. It's ok—good, actually—to cry and acknowledge the loss. Remember the good times and how that person's friendship influenced your life for the better.
3. Don't put too much emotional weight on material things. Like us mortals, they are susceptible to damage and the strains of age. They can be easily lost through theft or fire or financial troubles. Remember that your own value is measured independently of your wealth. It doesn't go with you to the other side. God is not impressed by this wealth. Neither are His angels or your brethren in Heaven.
4. Do your part in protecting God's other creatures. God expects us to protect the least of his creatures. He put us in charge of His earthly realm with the command that we would be good stewards. There is no glory in hunting for sport or razing mountains or drilling in the ancient glaciers.

5. Spread the Good News so that everyone you meet might have the chance to have eternal life in Heaven. If you truly believe that there is a Heaven and that there is but one way in, what does it say if you keep it a secret? The strongest advocates of God's kingdom were once his severest persecutors. Saint Paul instantly comes to mind. The best way to spread the Gospel—the Good Spell—is to live an honourable life and be a Believer of character. Your actions, your compassion and concern for others, along with your adherence to God's Word, will win the hearts of doubters. Non-Christians are watching you closely; they are seeing how you carry yourself. Are you a reflection of Jesus? As Scripture says, *wherever your treasure is, there your heart and thoughts will be also (Matthew 6:22 NLT).*

6. Let your heart be completely in God's hands all your days. If you do this, He will help you through any loss, no matter how great.

My soul is weary with sorrow;
strengthen me according to your word
(Psalm 119:28 NIV).

27 PURPLE HEART:
"Courage"

Be brave. Be Bold. In all you do.

Few people in life are given a credible soapbox; you must nevertheless find and deliver your own voice. The world is full of those living 'lives of quiet desperation.' There is no faster way to get there than to squelch your voice and remain silent your whole life.

There will always be those who are given a stage but have nothing useful to say. At best, they are a distraction, an irritant, and a reminder that they are taking the place of someone who has something positive to say. And, maybe that someone is you.

At worst, they encourage others in the same vein with a message and a style that are against all that is good.

Some people, you have noticed, are born yellers. Vocal to the core. They look for the mountain to pitch their cause. They stretch the truth to suit their need. They raise their voice until they are the only ones who can be heard.

That is when courage is required. That is when you must stand up and be heard. Though it will seem like it, you will of course never be alone. The Holy Spirit is within you and is there to give you the courage to find the strength to raise your voice so you will be heard.

Voices come in many tones. Speeches on a soapbox. Whispers in a beaten soul's ear. Silent prayers on bended knees.

Letters to the editor. Signed petitions. God's Word.

A raised hand. An arm around another's shoulder. A knock on a stranger's door.

Don't be intimidated by the multitude of life around you. Countless times, you will feel like the only fish swimming upstream. There is injustice all around us, and it should be bitter to your spirit. The inhumanity of humanity will give you many a sad day, and it will be the courage of another whispering in your ear that will raise your spirits. God's angels are all around you, and they will encourage you if you learn to recognize them.

Be bold in life. Make your own soapbox, whatever that may be, and stand tall upon it. Speak in clarity, with honour and love.

Try always to do what is right in God's eyes. The key word is 'try.' You will not be successful at all times, but God loves an honest heart. He knows what is kept inside of it, and He smiles when you are bold in His name.

Courage, though, is never free. Nor is freedom. There is always a price. But, you know, there is a price when you do nothing as well. If you wait for the next man to speak, and he doesn't, then an opportunity is lost. And, sometimes, we only get one chance.

Be wise, though, in your courage. Choose your battles well. Likewise, choose your allies with care and caution.

Know their hearts as best you can. Understand what motivates them. Are they genuine? Are they in it for the right reasons? Is their heart with God?

Question all things until you are sure of the answers. Watch for the sense of false security. It will be the Devil's way to keep you quiet.

Don't hide your light under the bushel. Keep the candle in your hand so that you will stay on the straight path, and will draw others onto the path with you. There is strength in numbers, and God desires that we would all be saved and brought safely then to Heaven. Where, for once and for all, the impurities of our character will be left behind and we will shine far brighter than ever before.

But life, like courage, is action in the here and now. Be bold. For God. Your family and friends. Strangers. The oppressed. The innocent. And yourself.

Act with courage,
and may the Lord be with those who do well
(2 Chronicles 19:11 NIV).

28 INDIGO:
"Prayer"

When I was little, I used to kneel beside my bed and pray. That was after I had checked for dragons in the closet and monsters under the bed. They were never there, of course, but I looked every night anyway. And I prayed to God even when I didn't have much to say.

I was raised an Episcopalian. Growing up, the focus seemed to be on our *Book of Common Prayer*. At my confirmation I received my own *Book of Common Prayer* for our Bishop and our Rector to sign. I have it to this day.

In the Episcopal Church, the first thing you do when you come in to church is to kneel and pray. It is also the last thing you do before you leave. The service itself includes a lot of prayer time. Before the late seventies, the service every other Sunday was known as Morning Prayer.

The prayers, though beautiful in language, are recited in unison. There is no spontaneity or shading that comes from the heart. Even grace, when we said it at meals, was a canned phrase or two. Despite converting to the Baptist faith over fifteen years ago, I still find it uncomfortable to pray aloud for others within a small group.

I find it ironic with the Episcopal Church that a church that so devotes itself to prayer should, in fact, raise children to be uncomfortable with praying.

What, then, is prayer? Simply communicating with God, from our spirit to His—and not just to ask for things either. There is nothing to be afraid of or embarrassed. It is a truly awesome feeling, though, to realize that you are literally talking with the Creator of the Universe. To recognize that, in addition to keeping all that is 'going,' He would have time to listen to our petty concerns.

That is the key, though. God is patient, and He is able to appreciate that the fears and concerns and desires of us mortals are magnified in our minds. We worry, even though He tells us we shouldn't. We panic, when we should relax and trust Him. We crave earthly pleasures, rather than focus on our eternal souls.

Yet God still loves us despite these failings. Amazingly, He doesn't hold a grudge when days or weeks go by between our prayers to Him. He doesn't give us a cold shoulder when every prayer is a request for a special favour. Or when we ask for forgiveness for the eighty-third time.

Instead, our loving father in Heaven, is at our beck and call. Twenty-four-seven. He is like a father waiting at the side of the pool while his young one tries to swim. He watches intently, ready to jump in at the first call.

Prayer, then, is talking with God. Quietly or aloud; alone or in a group. It is a two-way conversation but to hear Him, your heart must be quiet. He speaks through the heart, directly to your spirit—the spirit that was awakened in you when you accepted Christ.

When should we pray? Daily, and often.

Devote yourselves to prayer with an alert mind and a thankful heart (Colossians 4:2 NLT). Speak to Him with a sincere heart.

If only you would prepare your heart and lift up your hands to him in prayer! (Job 11:13 NLT).

Be joyful always; pray continually; give thanks in all circumstances, for this is God's will for you in Christ Jesus. (1 Thessalonians 5:16 NIV).

How should we pray? With humility and sincerity.

When you pray, go into your room, close the door and pray to your Father, who is unseen. Then your Father, who sees what is done in secret, will reward you. And when you pray, do not keep on babbling like pagans, for they think they will be heard because of their many words. Do not be like them, for your Father knows what you need before you ask him (Matthew 6:6-7 NIV).

The key to prayer is a close relationship with God. If you are right with Him, you will pray often. It will seem a natural thing to do. You will not be like Adam and Eve hiding from God in the bushes. But were they ashamed that they were naked, or that had disobeyed God?

Sin separates us from God; it creates a barrier between our spirit and His. It prevents us from communicating with the One who made us.

Pray constantly for God's wisdom and guidance that you would stay on the right path, His path.

When your spirit feels tempted, call on God for help. Pray to Him. When you are hungry or lost, pray to Him for sustenance and direction.

When He saves you and blesses you, pray to Him. Give Him your praise in thanksgiving. Acknowledge that all good things come from Him.

When you make a mistake, as will happen, pray to God for forgiveness.

Pray often. And listen well.

Do not be anxious about anything, but in everything,
by prayer and petition, with thanksgiving,
present your requests to God
(Philippians 4:6 NIV).

29 GOLDENROD:
"Faith"

For a human being, one of the hardest things is to believe in something you cannot see or touch. Or something no one else has ever seen or touched.

When God gave us a mind of our own, He meant for it to be our own, stubborn nooks and all.

There are two types of faith. In the first case, I have faith—or confidence—that you, my children, will succeed. I have seen first-hand how hard you work. Your past performance gives me the confidence to believe that you will do well that which is already set firmly in your heart. I have faith in you.

There is risk at times with this kind of faith because it is dependent on mortal will. Like it or not, we cannot control our destiny. As much as I may believe you want to win a race, and no matter how fast you may be, there could be someone faster than you in the race. You could trip; your legs could give out. It just may not be your day to win.

The second type is blind faith. It can seem the riskier of the two because here you are placing all your hope on something you cannot physically touch or visually see. In a masterful quirk that only God could design, this faith—our faith in Him—is the only sure-fire way to win.

The closer door is not always the right way, or the surest way home.

One of our failings as mortal beings is our need to touch everything. You will see that the first time you take one of your children into a store. May it not be a shop of breakables!

We are tactile creatures. Even in the womb our hands are moving about and touching our surroundings. Always touching; always wanting to put things in our mouths. That was certainly Eve's problem. Imagine how different humanity would be today if she had left well enough alone.

Our eyes, the windows to our soul, can mislead us sometimes. Remember that. Just because something, or someone, is beautiful doesn't make it so. And just because you can't see something in front of you doesn't make it not exist.

God is real. He does exist. The moment you accept Christ, the minute you knock on the door you cannot see, He opens and enters into your heart. Yes, you knock, and He enters. Remember, God doesn't think the way we do. That is why Jesus was often so misunderstood by people who did see his miracles and who did touch Him and who did know, without a doubt, that He was God's Son.

Remember how He said *Blessed are the poor in spirit, for theirs is the kingdom of heaven"* (Matthew 5:3 NIV) and *Blessed are the meek, for they will inherit the earth (Matthew 5:5 NIV)*. The first shall be last and the last, first.

Jesus turned over the money-changers' table and at the same time turned our previous understanding upside-down. He came here not to establish an earthly kingdom, but a

Heavenly one. Not one that could be destroyed, but an eternal realm. Concepts difficult for us mortals to understand. Harder still to understand that our mortal flesh carries within it our eternal soul.

We must seek Him, not the other way around, but the moment we knock, the minute we ask, He answers. Once in our heart, He makes us His own forever. We are a new lamb in His flock, for all eternity. And from then on, His Spirit lives in us and strengthens our own. It gives our soul an eternal life and an external perspective. This eternal perspective is our faith.

Anyone who has accepted Christ knows instantly that they are forever changed, that they are no longer alone on this crazy planet. It is an incredible feeling to know we are part of the Creator's kingdom, a part of His plan.

This is not to say that your acceptance of Christ will preserve you from all adversity or feelings of loneliness. You are saved but you still have to get through this world in God's timing. He needs us here to spread His kingdom and do His work so that others might also be saved.

God is with you; you are not alone, and He will equip you as needed and protect you in His way, to His purpose.

Rare is the crayon that is returned to the box in the condition that it left. It will be worn and its wrapper torn. Some will be broken, held together by that same worn wrapper. Others will be but half their original size.

Saddest are the ones that never return. These are the ones rejected by the Master because they rejected Him. God is gracious; He always lets us take the first step, which, as with babies, is the most important one. And, as with any loving parent, He waits to catch us with open arms.

If only goodness walked the Earth, life would not be so disheartening. The secular world scoffs at the idea of a Devil but from the Bible we know he is real, and it is his work to keep the flock of Christ from growing. His greatest weapon is doubt, and he sows it relentlessly. From his days in the Garden, he knows the weakness of man's willpower. He knows the corrosive power of pride, lust, greed, among others. He uses it effectively to build hate and hostility among and with the different peoples of the world. He flames the torches of war in dramatic and destructive ways.

In less noticeable ways, the Devil whispers in our ear to shake our faith. He encourages the world to abandon our faith and our God. He encourages us to live for the moment, to seek pleasure first, and to put ourselves above all others, including God.

As humans we walk a fine line to have enough confidence to put our trust in God, yet not so much confidence to believe we can survive on our own. Not enough confidence—a lack of faith—and we fall prey to the Evil One who waits in the bushes and low places.

Throughout your life you will meet many nay-sayers and Doubting Thomas's who will, quite frankly, be jealous of your strong faith. Do not waver or look back. Pray to our Father in Heaven that He would give you strength, as well as wisdom. If it is His will, He will use this time to work in that person's own heart. The mortal enemy of Christ today could be another St. Paul in a future day.

Stand firm for Christ. Stay strong in your faith. No one has ever touched a rainbow but we know they're real. You can't touch the air, but it's real and sustains you in life.

Likewise, faith is the oxygen that sustains your spirit, and we know from Scripture that *it is impossible to please God without faith. Anyone who wants to come to him must believe that God exists and that he rewards those who sincerely seek him (Hebrews 11:6 NLT).*

Here is another verse of Scripture that sums it best*: By faith we understand that the entire universe was formed at God's command, that what we now see did not come from anything that can be seen (Hebrews 11:3 NLT).*

As a much younger saying says, "Seeing is not believing; believing is seeing."

We are not called Believers for nothing. It is a recognition of our faith, of our absolute trust in an all-powerful, all-knowing God. Whenever another soul crosses the threshold of faith and joins the flock of Believers, all the angels in Heaven dance, and the Lord God is yet again pleased.

As you do not know the path of the wind,
or how a body is formed in a mother's womb,
so you cannot understand the work of God,
the Maker of all things
(Ecclesiastes 11:5 NIV).

TIMOTHY RAY PHILLIPS

30 SEPIA:

"Memories"

One of our most precious gifts is memory, the ability to freeze moments of our lives and store them in our mental vault. To be replayed at will in the future. It is, of course, a double-edged sword: some memories are better left alone and, of course, over time, as with real film, the image is never quite as clear or true-to-life.

Without memories, we would never learn. We would continue to touch a hot stove over and over until our eighty-seventh year of life. We would wonder about the blisters on our hand but never make the connection to the hot surface.

We use memory to learn from our mistakes. We recall what worked before and what didn't. We make slight changes, try again, and compare the results to the image in our memory. Without memory, we would still be living in dark caves outside the Garden of Eden.

We build relationships, memory by memory. The mental collection of events gets us through the difficult times.

They enable us to build trust in our fellow men, and, more importantly, retain God's love and embrace the Gospel.

Even happy memories, though, can be bittersweet. Who would ever want to miss seeing his child take her first step? There is such joy in watching your little one who, not so long ago was confined to a crib, build up the courage to stand and take a step all on her own. You take it all in and file it away in your memory bank.

The years pass quickly—too quickly—and she is suddenly in Middle School. You superimpose the memory of her first steps as she runs across the street to school, and immediately a sadness of sorts enters your heart. You are reminded that while you have gained a young girl, you have lost a baby.

Every day is like that, though most people rarely think of it that way. As your children fall asleep each night, in some way they die—never again to be that exact age again. Hours later, they awake as a new person ready for a new day, and you have been blessed anew.

Our lives end at the end of each day, and a new one begins when we wake up the next morning. We are different: refreshed and, happily, somewhat wiser and better focused and enhanced with more memories processed overnight. All to carry us through the new day.

You will find that the older you get, the faster the days will fly by, and the shorter the restless nights. Stay alert throughout your life; make memories by day. Remember that sometimes it is the 'insignificant' moments that make the most powerful, life-changing moments. They will also be the memories you miss the most—that is, the ones you wish you could re-live.

Sometimes a memory is nothing more than a smell. Those are the quickest ones to be re-awakened—years and years later. Sometimes a memory is as short as a second. Sometimes it is just a feeling, intense and indescribable wrapped in a coating of nostalgia.

Memories can be good or bad, pleasant or painful, helpful or harmful. My best advice to you is to let go of the bad memories. Don't let them stay too long in your mind or you may risk not being able to erase them completely. They are not healthy to your spirit and are most likely an indicator of unfinished business.

Most likely, you have not dealt with something or someone directly. Forgive the person, as you would want them to forgive you. That's pretty basic, I know, but it's in the Lord's Prayer for a good reason. You cannot grow in your spirit if you are weighed down by such baggage. Where we are going, luggage is not allowed, so you might as well leave it behind now and save yourself the burden of carrying it around. If you do, I guarantee you will be a whole lot happier today, and your memories of this day will be worthy of a follower of Christ.

You are the master of your memory archive. Enjoy the most out of each day that God gives you. Make great memories. Learn from them and think back on them so that you never forget the experiences that God has allowed you to have.

Bad things will happen. Evil will be done to you. Lean on the Holy Spirit within you to see you through. Learn from it. Seek forgiveness when you commit a wrong. Give forgiveness when it is sought. Then let it go, and give thanks to God for seeing you through another day and giving you the fun and adventure of that day.

The world is a doubting place, with enough cynicism to fill an ocean or two. Let your soul and spirit be an island of great memories worthy of a Believer in a life pure and everlasting.

The memory of the righteous will be a blessing
(Proverbs 10:7 NIV).

31 MAROON:
"Reflection"

What do you see when you look at yourself in the mirror? What do you think God sees when he looks into your spirit?

We are an open book to Him, the Creator. We are so used to the idea that no one can read our minds and, therefore, our true feelings and motives. Sometimes, we can even hide it from ourselves. People can go for years denying what is by then so obvious to everyone else around them. Often, others notice you are in love before you do, or they recognize your passion for something before you see it yourself.

On the other hand, we often expect people to know our true honourable intentions assuming that we are in fact an open book.

As you have probably figured out by now, nothing involving mind or emotion is that simple. You cannot assume on the one hand that your inner thoughts are untouchable—even by God—and, on the other hand, your actions and unspoken words will be understood in the way you would hope.

Throughout your life, even if you are honourable to the bare bone, you will be misunderstood, and good deeds will be seen as part of a hidden agenda. That is a characteristic of man. It is a part of the survival of the fittest. Abel lacked that, and didn't see his brother Cain's murderous intent. He paid the price for that, though. Since then men have become more suspicious of each other, even their fellow brothers.

This natural suspicion is now part of our collective DNA just as birds know their migratory paths without having their parents around to show them the way. Sadly, it's a more jaded way to go through life. The harsh realities of our mortal world, though, only reinforce the merits of staying aloof and keeping your hands in your pockets when you're in the city or an unfamiliar neighbourhood.

Besides affecting the quality of this life, such a cynical attitude makes it more difficult to share the Good News of Christ with others. They are half expecting you to fleece them in some way.

God knows this, though, which is why He tells us to let His light shine upon us so that others might see the goodness and be drawn towards us and, thereby, Him. He knows we all live in a dark world, which is why He instructs us to put our light on top of the bushel, not under it.

He also expects us to live a life that is honourable and pleasing to Him so that the light will reflect that very goodness that is within us. In Acts 13:47 Jesus says *I have made you a light for the Gentiles that you may bring salvation to the ends of the earth (NIV).*

It is all about furthering His kingdom. It always has been, and always will be.

The Bible asks and answers an important question: *How does a young man keep his ways pure? By living according to His Word (Psalm 119:9 NIV).* I have tried in this short book to highlight the importance of God in our lives, and the relevance of His Word in keeping us grounded spiritually.

One thing is clear. You cannot have a reflection without light. Peer into a lake on a moonless night, and you will see nothing on the surface but dark ink. Stand in front of the mirror in an unlit room, and you will see only a black wall.

The moon shines as a reflection of the sun from the other side of the Earth. Think about it: the moonlight of tonight is the result of tomorrow's day. Without a tomorrow, there is no possibility to reflect on today.

As Believers, we know that *God is light; in Him there is no darkness at all. If we claim to have fellowship with Him yet walk in the darkness, we lie and do not live by the truth (1 John 1:5-6 NIV).*

Think of it this way: We were created in God's image (Old Testament) to grow the body of Christ (New Testament). We are to reflect the love of Jesus. To be that reflection you need God's light to be the centre of your life.

Of course, you are smart and know by now that reflection also occurs inside us. That is possible because *God made his light shine in our hearts to give us the light of the knowledge of the glory of God in the face of Christ. (2 Corinthians 4:6 NIV).* It is not about our physical looks. It has always been about our spirit—not the soul or the body.

God's greatest desire is that all our spirits would be in perfect communion with Him. He wants everyone to come into His circle. It is the only non-exclusive club in the universe.

We are all on a journey of faith from the day we are born until we cross the threshold to the other side, where the light is strong and pure. We walk through valleys of darkness, and the only way to keep from stumbling or straying off course is to keep the pathway lit. Each of us plays an important part in that. When we reflect the love of God and righteous living, we guide others along the path. We encourage those who are unsure of the way or are weary from the hardships of our difficult mortal lives.

Make a difference with your life. An eternal difference. Reflect God in all you do. Let His Spirit fully work in and through you so that you will be a joy to others. This is not a small task, but a worthy and honourable one.

As water reflects a face,
so a man's heart reflects the man
(Proverbs 27:19 NIV).

32 Violet:

"Passion"

We live such a short time as mortals. We must gather up our learning as quickly as possible so that we can get on with our lives and really live. Before we turn to dust.

There is no time to dally, to mark time and ponder what you should do with your life. Likewise, there is no time to settle for the ordinary. By the time you are middle-aged, if you have opted for the safe zone, you will very much regret it. That route is the way to a mid-life crisis, and then you will spend your remaining years grumbling about the 'lost years.'

The solution is actually pretty simple. In all you do, do it with passion. Learn to read your passion. Before you get involved in something, take time to ask whether it is a worthwhile endeavour. Is it pleasing to God? Will it make a positive difference in the world? If you answer, 'yes,' then jump in with both feet bare. Feel the crushed grapes between your toes.

If you are passionate about something, you will know it, and so will others around you. It will be apparent in the tone of your voice and the movement of your hands.

Be passionate for the Lord.

Be passionate with your spouse.

Be passionate in raising your children and loving them.

Never take these three for granted. You were created for them, and they will be your biggest allies and fans in life. And, despite the finite dimension of life, any mark of time can seem monotonously slow when you are alone.

Be passionate about your work. We were created to work—to serve God and to glorify Him. He has blessed each of us with unique talents and desires. Use those gifts in a way that brings you real happiness.

For me, I am passionate about my writing. When I am immersed in a poem or a story, I am just that—immersed. It protects me from the ordinary. When I am most stressed at work, that is when I am most creative in my writing. It is a release valve. A counter-balance to working with numbers all day. For us accountants, balance is everything.

In my life I have met and interviewed many people who have found themselves 'stuck' in a career path, and it shows on their faces. Such misery at a young age. We are all presented with a significant fork in the road early in our lives. Probably the most common question asked of children is 'What do you want to be when you grow up?' The most common answer is a shrug, followed by 'I don't know.' Unless, you are asking an eight year old, in which case, he will probably say 'an astronaut.' Or, your brother Patrick's case, 'a pizza deliveryman or a cartographer.' An odd response unless you consider that deliverymen need good maps.

As a parent, one of the best pieces of advice I can give to my children is to make sure they stay passionate in all they do. When the passion is gone, you have to ask 'What changed?' Never just keep going. If you are not in love with what you are doing, you have to find out why, and then correct your course.

I said earlier that you must jump in with both feet. Implicit in that command is the logic that you must look where you are leaping. If a cliff is a few feet ahead, oh boy.

Do your homework. Make sure that the cause justifies your involvement. Read between the lines; read the fine print. Question things that seem too good to be true; they generally are. Ask yourself the important question: Is the endeavour worthy of God? Is it true to God's Word as written in the Bible? If you have an odd, unsettling feeling about it, chances are it isn't worthy. The spirit inside you can sense falseness.

On the other hand, if it feels right (to the spirit, not the flesh), then roll up your sleeves and delve into it with all your soul. If you do this, you will look back on your life and be pleased. And, God will be pleased. And that is all that really counts.

Passion equals life. A life well-lived. I remember a sermon from our pastor when he quoted from Revelations 3:16. His main point was that God prefers the extreme. There is value in being either hot or cold (medicinal hot springs or refreshing drink); lukewarm water provides neither.

Passion is in the extreme. The ordinary is in the lukewarm. Anyone can be ordinary. You can be ordinary without even trying.

Make a difference in the world. Have an impact and have fun in doing it. And, when you do, as you pass the gates into Heaven, you will hear those most comforting words, "Well done, my good and faithful servant."

He dressed in Righteousness,
put it on like a suit of armour,
with Salvation on his head like a helmet,
put on Judgment like an overcoat
and threw a cloak of Passion across his shoulders
(Isaiah 59:17 Message).

33 FOREST GREEN:
"Stewardship"

God. The Creator of the Universe. I marvel at His imagination. He gave each species a brain and a heart and a stomach. From there, it is all fair game. Long necks and African-shaped ears. Turtle shell and kangaroo pouch. Humps and double-humps. Flying squirrels and prolific mice. Coiled snakes and upside-down bats. Hippos and Rhinos. Fast cats and bloodhounds. Frogs and pigs; bears and hares.

Octopus and walrus. Penguins and flying fish. Jellyfish and oyster. Sturgis and cod. Lobster, shrimp and other pods. Seahorse. Blue whale and minnow. Stingrays and bat rays. Dolphin and shark. Light and dark.

Birds of every shape and size and colour. The thumb-sized hummingbird and the Ostrich. Hawk and duck. Flamingo and pheasant. Pigeon and grouse. Cardinal and the golden goose. Owl and lark. Stork and swan. And the sparrow whom God cares for every day.

Butterflies of every colour, and ants, red and black. Ladybugs and fireflies. Bees and yellow jackets. Black widows and tarantulas. Fleas and flies. Crickets and cicadas. Ticks and termites. Worms and earwigs. Bugs that bite; bugs that build. Moths that eat away what man has made.

Flowers to match the butterflies in beauty. Towering trees. Redwoods and oak. Birch and maple. Weeping willows. Blue spruce and the evergreens. Moss and ferns. English ivy and Bermuda grass. Grapes and barley. Orange and cherry. Oat and wheat; corn and soy. And all the weeds that crowd the beds.

Mountains and hills. Rainforest and desert. Savannah and tundra. Alpine and meadowland. The Plains and the Steppes. Deltas and plateaus. Forest and chaparral. The North Pole and the South.

Winter and Summer. Spring and Fall. Rain, wind, and snow. Sun and moon and stars. Blue sky and cloud. Morning mist and night fog. Salty spray and clover breeze. Thunderstorm and sandstorm. Shooting stars and Northern Lights. Lightning and rainbows. Cold drizzle and tropic steam.

God made all things, and He calls on us all to keep it clean and safe. Preserve the land. Protect the animals. Enjoy the world. Leave it better than you found it.

Most of all, marvel at the playfulness of God and His resourcefulness in creating such a diverse world. He knows us well, and how easily bored we become with life. He put great excitement into the world to keep us engaged, intrigued, and most of all, amused.

I believe it breaks God's heart each time one of His creations is the last of its kind to leave the Earth.

In your life you will be given many things to love and watch over. A spouse, children, family, friends, neighbours, co-workers. Puppies and goldfish. Parakeets and rabbits.

And the occasional cat that strays into your yard.   Now and then, when you can, leave a saucer of milk on the porch. It will give God a smile and it isn't half-bad for the cat either.

But ask the animals, and they will teach you,
or the birds of the air, and they will tell you;
or speak to the earth, and it will teach you,
or let the fish of the sea inform you.
Which of all these does not know
that the hand of the Lord has done this?
In his hand is the life of every creature,
and the breath of all mankind
(Job 12:7-10 NIV).

TIMOTHY RAY PHILLIPS

34 Midnight Blue:
"Solitude"

Every now and then, grab a hammock and swing in the shade for a bit. Lose an afternoon to yourself or spend a night in a tree house ten feet from the ground.

It will do you good. Every day, everyone is telling you what to do. Your mother and I; your teachers; your friends. Someday, your boss and, of course, the Government. And, when you are married, and God-willing, blessed with children, you will feel even more pressed at times. It is then that you must give yourself a break in the shade.

You must learn to step inside your own space where you can take the time to think it through and sort it all out so that it makes sense to you.

We all need our quiet time from time to time. Whether we curl up with our favourite blankey or a good book, or take a long walk along the beach.

And in those quiet moments, listen closely and you will hear God speaking to you. He is patient, and waits until you are alone to speak. He wants your full attention for what He says is worth hearing with a clear mind and a clean heart.

Never fear solitude. Embrace it and enjoy it. In this busy world, the quiet moments can become few and far between if you are not careful.

Lay on a grassy hill and watch the stars. The same God that made them, made you.

Walk in a field with the fireflies. The same God made us all.

Sit among the wildflowers and watch the bees and butterflies at work. Even when we are at rest, the world goes on. It is like a merry-go-round, and sometimes you need to jump off and let the world spin without you for a spell.

Then, when you are ready to get back in, take a deep breath, jump aboard, and hold on tight. And remember to have a good time!

But Jesus often withdrew
to lonely places and prayed
(Luke 5:16 NIV).

35 COPPER:

"Tithing"

Jesus said it is easier for a camel to go through the eye of a needle than it is for a rich man to get into Heaven.

We cling to the material things of life. Houses, cars, toys, gadgets, bank accounts. We all do; it is a carryover from our first days in the sandbox. Remember the boy with the shovel? Nothing was going to get him to share. Nothing. Not even Mom.

As we grow up, we collect more things. More stuff. Boxes and boxes of stuff. Never in the history of Man have more in society had the ability to collect stuff beyond their dreams.

One of my touchstone Bible verses is Matthew 6:19: *Don't store up treasures here on Earth, where they can be eaten by moths and get rusty, and where thieves break in and steal. Store your treasures in heaven....Wherever your treasure is, there your heart and thoughts will be also (NLT).* And, a little later in Matthew 6:24: *You cannot serve both God and money (NLT).*

The Bible says we should not worry about everyday life, and yet we do. Like the ant, we horde and save beyond what is needed for the rainy day. At some point, we pass the line between wise saving (good stewardship) and greed. That insatiable desire to have more and more material things at the expense of our spiritual health. As the Bible says, a person cannot serve both God and money. The spiritual realm or the earthly one.

All good things come from God. The gift of health and of work. God provides. To return a tithe, a tenth, of what we earn is to acknowledge God as the source of these good things. It is a measure of discipline to strengthen our spirit and to remind us that, of the two, God is mightier than money. God is our Master, our true King. Money, on the other hand, is an invention of Man.

Even more importantly, tithing allows the Church to help those who are in need, believers and non-believers alike. It furthers God's Kingdom by supporting missionaries, caring for the elderly and the orphans, feeding the homeless, and winning new hearts for the Lord.

Tithe in the three T's. I call it the trinity. Your treasure, your talent, and your time. It is not enough to put a check in the offering plate. Use the gifts that God has given you to help in any way you can. Help in the Church. The community. The school. If you are pure in purpose, the love you have for Christ will shine brightly, and others will notice. They will be drawn to the light inside, and you may be able to lead someone to Christ.

What greater reward for you in Heaven than to see a familiar face there by the grace of God working through you. You will have helped to give them an eternal life with

God, and that is a reward that moths, or rust, or thieves can never take away.

Use your money wisely in life; be a good steward with what the Lord has given you. But keep a tender heart and be moved to give. Often and generously.

The Lord expects no less.

A tithe of everything from the land,
whether grain from the soil
or fruit from the trees,
belongs to the Lord; it is holy to the Lord
(Leviticus 27:30 NIV).

TIMOTHY RAY PHILLIPS

36 MAGENTA:

"Poetry"

I wrote my first poem when I was thirteen. It was about a bird, and it was awful. Cornier than the state of Iowa and that, in itself, is pretty corny.

I focused on the rhyme, forced the words to fit and in the process I filled it with sap. It had no relevance to a thirteen-year-old's world. There was no angst, no wonder, no marvel. It was awful.

But. There is always a *but*, isn't there? But at the time, and that is what matters, I felt good when I finished it and showed it to others and when the local paper printed it, it encouraged me to keep writing. And, over the years, poem by poem, I got better at it.

That is not to say that I don't still write the clunkers, though I hope they are fewer and farther in between. I have developed an inner ear for the language—I can sense when it feels natural. That is my yardstick for any poem. It must feel genuine.

I give more weight to the rhythm than I do the rhyme. When I focus that way, I find the natural rhymes and the play on words, fall into place.

I also write about things I know and things I have felt. My daily life gives rise to my poems.

I don't rush them. I let them rest in my brain for as long as they need. But I know that they are there. I will have an experience or hear a phrase that triggers a thought and I will know that it is the start of a poem. It may rush out in full force that very night when I cannot sleep, or it may lie dormant for a year or more.

But why worry? I know it will come when it is time.

Why poetry, Papa? Why do you write at all?

For me, ever since I can remember, I have been drawn to writing. It is my voice, my little soapbox on a corner of the Earth.

Life, as you are learning already, is pretty stressful at times. There is so much you want to change, but can't. The forces against it are too great, too many. There are many men behind many curtains, and no one will tell you who is really pulling the levers.

In this, I believe there are four types of people. Those who write in poetry, those who write in facts, those who read what others write, and those who cannot read at all. My heart is with the writers, especially the poets. They are the ones who want to sit by the stream and dream; they want nothing ill to happen in the world. I am partial to the Poets because they would run to Heaven tonight if the gates were suddenly opened. There is a strain in their hearts because all is not right with the world, and they know it. But they write about the way it could be, if only Man had not fallen.

The factual writers, God bless them, see the world in more real terms. Things are black and white. They go about life happily. It is what it is. Good, bad, and ugly. In stark terms, with lots of facts and figures. It all seems so clinical at times. It is as if they accept the way things are in some respects.

Genocide. How is it possible that someone could have found a single word to describe such a horrible act? And, yet, somebody did.

Poetry is not all about words. It is how you live. Do you create things of beauty? Do you bring light into areas that are dark? Do you lead your life with grace and compassion?

Be a Poet. Don't worry about the rhyming. Learn to feel the rhythm that is within your spirit. When you colour, go outside the lines. And when you find an odd play on words, rejoice in the moment, and thank God that He has given you the gift to create. For all good things really are a gift from God.

Pleasant words are a honeycomb,
sweet to the soul and healing to the bones
(Proverbs 16:24 NIV).

TIMOTHY RAY PHILLIPS

37 SILVER:
"Respect"

As a society, we live with a set of established rules. Some are in writing (laws); others are based on things that have evolved over time (traditions). Yet others are based on our core values which, as Believers, are contained and explained and illumined in the Bible.

Clearly, laws can be changed. At one time women and minorities were not allowed to vote; at one time it was illegal to drink alcohol, regardless of your age.

Traditions also change. Some families open presents on Christmas morning; others on Christmas Eve. One approach is not better than the other; they are just different ways to celebrate the gift of Christ. There is comfort in traditions and when you marry it is likely that your spouse's traditions will differ from yours. Together, though, you will find compromises that at first will seem strange because they are new. Over time, they will become your traditions and the ones your kids will bring into their marriage.

What about our core values as Believers? Can they change? Some Christians take the Bible literally; others treat God's Word much more as guidelines to help steer them through a tricky and frightening world.

Respect happens when we give deference to something, whether it be a law, a tradition, a person, or a value. When we follow the law, we show respect to our fellow citizens. We also show respect to God's Word, which commands us to be good citizens in areas of earthly realm.

When we respect tradition, we show respect to our society, both to those who preceded us and those now living. Most traditions came to be as a way to bring a community or nation together, to provide a framework for men and women of free will to get along well with each other. The same is true for God's commandments contained in the Bible. They are His instructions to help ensure we live a good and prosperous life.

Respect is an acknowledgement that there is something greater than ourselves. For a human being, that can be a tough lump to swallow. Deep inside, there is a part in us that still holds fast to the idea that we could be mini-gods— masters of our own destiny. Our egos prevent us sometimes from admitting that laws should apply to all, including ourselves. Why else do people so easily cut in line or find the shadowy shortcuts? Why are we all so good at rationalizing those times we choose to ignore the law or, worse, God's Word?

Each person must decide the role of God's Word in their lives. I believe that decision process is part of our life-long walk with the Lord. For me, the Bible provides a message not only of love but consistency and respect. It outlines how we should live here on Earth and how we should treat others ("the Golden Rule"). And, most importantly, how we should relate to and respect the Almighty God.

We must defer to God in all things. We must respect Him and His Word with every cell of our soul. It is a consistent message from Genesis to Revelation: God is in control:

1. He created the Universe. One word, universe, He made everything.
2. He created us in His image.
3. He loves us despite our failings.
4. So much so that He came down to Earth as a man so he could truly walk in our shoes.
5. He died a cruel death in order to remove any separation (sin) between us and Him.
6. He lives among us today and is active in our lives.
7. In the future, His Son will come again and we will all be together in Heaven for all eternity.

Remember this as well:

Our entrance into Heaven is through Jesus and Jesus alone.

We are brought into Heaven through God's grace, not by our own merits.

God desires that all of His children know Him.

Therefore, we should spread God's message of love and redemption to everyone we meet.

Finally, and this is important: respect yourself. Throughout your life you will doubtless be challenged and urged by others to question your own worth, as well as your faith in God. Be strong in your faith. Respect the strength of your convictions and your value to God. He loves you no matter what, just as your parents love you.

A good name is more desirable than great riches;
to be esteemed is better than silver or gold
(Proverbs 22:1 NIV).

38 CORNFLOWER:

"Kindness"

What kind of person do you want to be? Unlike the question, 'What do you want to be when you grow up?' you do not need to wait until you are eighteen to learn the answer. The qualities that are desirable in an adult are relevant to a Believing child.

It is interesting that in 2 Peter 1:5, the Bible shows an upward cascading relationship of Christian virtues, beginning with faith and ending with love. One quality leads to another until you are at that highest level—Love. A surrendering of your self-interests for the benefit of another person.

The Lord had given Moses and the Israelites the Ten Commandments to follow. Two *Do's* and eight *Don'ts;* all intended to help us show our love for God and our love for each other. However, man being man, we gradually expanded these *simple* ten Commandments into the 613 commandments (*mitzvot*, in Hebrew) recorded in the Old Testament. Of these, 248 (interestingly, the number of bones in the body according to rabbinic tradition) were *Do's* and 365 (the days in a year) were *Don'ts*.

As an accountant, I should note that we did the same thing with the US Tax Code. When the federal income tax began in 1913, a person's tax return fit on a single postcard and the Code itself was about four hundred pages. A hundred years later it was 73,954 pages, or 185 times the original set of rules. Complicating the Simple. It's what we do!

By the time Jesus came to Earth, the spirit of God's commandments (which were based on his love for us) had been lost to the rigid compliance of minutia. So Jesus did what He always did. He distilled the overly complex to the simple truth: *Love God. Love your neighbour.* He added *as you love yourself* because he knew and understood the innate selfishness of man.

So if love is the greatest of the virtues, kindness is the second:

LOVE
Kindness
Godliness
Perseverance
Self-Control
Knowledge
Goodness
Faith

These virtues, or qualities, are similar to the special gifts, or fruit of the Spirit, we receive once we are Believers. It is the Holy Spirit living within us that brings forth this fruit, and which empowers us and reflects the character of a strong Christian: love, joy, peace, patience, kindness, goodness, faithfulness, gentleness, and self-control.

Earlier, I made a distinction between our spirit and our soul. The importance is evident here, in our character. God, because He is God, is not capable of generating anything that is not good. His Holy Spirit is the incorruptible seed that is planted in our spirit when we accept Christ into our heart. God's Spirit dwelling within us awakens our once-dead spirit and begins a regeneration—a re-birth—of our own spirit. The goal is to have a healthy, eternal communion with God.

From the point of our acceptance, we are never alone again. Our clay-vessel bodies become walking, thinking lanterns holding the light of Christ. Along with the Spiritual fruit, our spirit is given a personal, unbreakable connection with the Creator of the Universe. That is a concept that if we truly understood its meaning our brains would freeze forever.

Our soul, though, is not infused with the Holy Spirit. It is the playing field for the Devil. It is our weak spot—our ego, longings, mortal appetites, area of doubts and worries. The Devil wants our soul, and it is the job of the *Spirit*-empowered spirit to bring the soul into submission, as it once was in the Garden.

We know from experience that it is a constant battle between soul and spirit. None of us, saints included, exhibit only the Spiritual fruit and nothing else. We all have moments of weakness where the soul prevails. We all know Christians who can be unkind at times, or petty, selfish, dishonest, catty, lustful, conceited, and such. How is that possible if they are filled with the Holy Spirit? You and I are Believers and yet we do not always reflect the good fruit.

How is that possible? This is an important question and often asked by non-believers as support for not joining those "hypocritical Christians."

The Devil uses our humanity to try to limit the growth of God's kingdom. He works on the pride of our soul to keep the spirit within us at arm's length. It is a battle royal raging inside us. Even though we are Believers, we are not perfectly in tune with our spirit the second we accepted Christ. Although our victory over death (of our body) is assured, we are nevertheless on a long, sometimes difficult journey to reach the point where our spirit is again in control of our soul and body. In other words, that perfect equilibrium that existed in Adam and Eve before the Fall.

So what exactly is kindness, other than being an important fruit of the Spirit? It is a real interest in caring for those around you, but it does not come naturally to us. Sharing, lending a hand, letting others go first, is a godly trait, not a human one. Sometimes it takes real effort to be kind, particularly to those who have hurt you in the past.

I like what the Lord says in Galatians 6:8-9: *The one who sows to please the Spirit, from the Spirit will reap eternal life. Let us not become weary in doing good, for at the proper time we will reap a harvest if we do not give up. Therefore, as we have the opportunity, let us do good to all people, especially to those who belong to the family of believers (NIV).*

God knows that doing your best to follow in His footsteps is difficult and tiresome for the mortal race. It is not enough to have His Holy Spirit dwelling within us. We must allow ourselves to be changed by the Spirit. We must quiet our soul—the unheard chattering that exists in our mind, so that we can hear the whispering of the Spirit.

Rarely does it yell. It speaks in a calming voice on a different wavelength altogether.

People can go years without hearing the Lord speak. Others hear Him all the time. The difference is in the reception given to the Holy Spirit by our own spirit. I need to be clear in this area. Many confuse good works with acceptance into Heaven. That is a great falsehood. Acceptance to Heaven comes from our acceptance of Jesus and His Spirit into our heart.

What follows, if you are obedient to the Spirit, is the Spiritual fruit. In other words, the good works (goodness, kindness, love) are evidence of your growth, not your future entrance into Heaven. This point is extremely important because many people see it in reverse order. The danger in doing that is that it replaces God's mercy with mortal effort, and there isn't enough time, talent, or goodness in Man to do the job that Jesus did on the cross.

Believing that it is our works, our good deeds, that gets us into Heaven is to say we do not need God's grace. We can do it all on our own. When you hear that, you should know it is your soul, not your spirit, that is speaking for you. If you hear yourself saying such things, stop in your tracks, pray to God for wisdom and knowledge of His truth, and then be quiet and listen for His Spirit to answer you.

Show kindness; be a kind person. Not for glory's sake but because in showing kindness to others you will be reflecting God's Spirit within you, and will do much to spread God's love. The fruit of your kindness to others may very well become the seed that will yield a new Believer where none existed.

Just as you should not hide your light under a bushel, you shouldn't keep the fruit inside you. Share it with others and let the Spirit move. In this way you will be fulfilling the Great Commission and spreading the Good News to others.

Make every effort to add to your faith goodness;
and to goodness, knowledge; and to knowledge,
self-control; and to self-control, perseverance;
and to perseverance, godliness; and to godliness,
brotherly kindness; and to brotherly kindness, love
(2 Peter 1:5 NIV).

39 Lavender:
"Compassion"

Compassion, I have been told, is not my strongest suit. It is appropriate then that this is among the last of the colours to be written.

Compassion is one of the more difficult of the spiritual fruits because it requires you to stand in the shoes of another and to understand emotionally what is coming over them. To be successful in this, you must have some knowledge of that person's life and how past events have affected them.

For me, I have always found it difficult to dwell on things—at least some things. My natural tendency is to move on. Fix what I can and try not to worry about the rest. This works if you can detach yourself emotionally. That, of course, causes other problems, often worse than not having compassion in the first place!

While I am continuing to struggle and grow in this area, I have learned a few things recently. First, be a good listener. Let the other person express themselves. Sit on your hands while they talk, if that is what it will take to keep you silent. As you listen, try to thread it through, to connect the dots, until you can fairly appreciate how the person is really feeling.

Listen with your eyes as well. If the person is truly in pain, sometimes words alone will not fully express it.

Ask how you can be supportive. It is great if you can figure it out on your own, but sometimes you have to ask.

Don't judge. Never try to solve the situation from your perspective. Often, the solution will not work anyway, and all you do is make the other person feel silly. Your friend will come to believe you don't really understand them. The value of a friendship is knowing that they see and appreciate you for who you already are.

Lend a hand or, better yet, a shoulder.

Continue to listen, and keep a clean handkerchief in your pocket.

If asked, give your opinion or suggestions but do so in a loving way, never forgetting that your friend or family is feeling hurt or alone or confused. Or angry, or any other emotion you can imagine. None of us is an open book, and we have no idea how the past has affected others. Often, we don't even know how we have ourselves been affected. Emotional time bombs can explode for an apparently unknown, or unrelated, reason.

Follow-through on your commitments. Life is for the long haul. There are few quick fixes in life.

Give hugs freely—and often.

Treat others with respect. Never knowingly hurt someone. Be a person of strength and integrity.

Never follow the crowd. Be a leader. Go out on a ledge to help another. Earn a reputation as a compassionate Believer, a true follower of Jesus Christ.

Perhaps most important, be still, pray, and listen to the spirit inside you for answers.

Know that we are all living in a difficult world in a finite period of time. All things, good and otherwise, will pass in time. No hurt lasts forever, so keep a perspective. Trust in God and know that He will never test you or put you in situations that you cannot handle.

The Earth is giant ark on a black sea. It is but a temporary refuge while our Father prepares a permanent place for us in Heaven. Keep that eternal perspective always in your mind.

In all things, in all places, at all times, remember that you are loved. You were created out of love, not dust alone, and we all thrive on love. When you see someone in pain, be compassionate and help as you can.

Listen with love. Speak with love and truth. Act with love. Give with love and grace.

And while you walk in another's shoes, have the courage to carry him if he needs it. A person is never too old for a piggy-back, especially from a good friend.

Therefore, as God's chosen people,
holy and dearly loved, clothe yourselves
with compassion, kindness, humility,
gentleness and patience
(Colossians 3:12 NIV).

TIMOTHY RAY PHILLIPS

40 PLUM:

"Generosity"

God loves a generous heart. He blesses those who give freely of their time, talent, and treasure to others less fortunate. If you consider what God has already given you, it should not be difficult to be a giving person in turn. He gave us a natural life in good health and a wealth of talent. He set us down in a colourful world of incredible diversity.

He created us with a good, strong family. He has blessed us to be bound by blood. Most importantly, He has bound us to His eternal kingdom through the shed blood of His most precious Son, Jesus. There is not a more generous gift He could have given. He has given us a full life, here on Earth and later in Heaven.

In this, God has set a model example. Jesus Himself said, in Matthew 25: 40-46:

The King will reply, 'I tell you the truth, whatever you did for one of the least of these brothers of mine, you did for me.'

Then he will say to those on his left, 'Depart from me, you who are cursed, into the eternal fire prepared for the

*devil and his angels. For I was hungry and you gave me
nothing to eat, I was thirsty and you gave me nothing to
drink, I was a stranger and you did not invite me in, I
needed clothes and you did not clothe me, I was sick and in
prison and you did not look after me.'*

*They also will answer, 'Lord, when did we see you hun-
gry or thirsty or a stranger or needing clothes or sick or in
prison, and did not help you?'*

"He will reply, 'I tell you the truth, whatever you did not
do for one of the least of these, you did not do for me.'

"Then they will go away to eternal punishment, but the
righteous to eternal life" (NIV).

The Lord's words are powerful, and I would not be honest if I told you that sharing generously comes naturally to
us all. It doesn't. From our first word—"Mine!"—it is a
struggle between our spirit, which seeks to be a copy and
shadow of God's love, and our soul, which struggles with
putting our individuality above all else. Oftentimes even at
the expense of God. It is a classic struggle waged by every
man, woman, and child who ever lived.

God gave us a free will at the very beginning, and our
souls intend to exercise it. Thus, selfishness—putting ourselves and our needs ahead of all others—is a natural be-
haviour. The more awkward path is to share freely the
various blessings given to us over the course of our natural
life. It is also the path God wants us to take.

From my own life experience I have observed one thing
about myself: when I consider the situation from an eternal
perspective, the importance of hanging on to my view dissipates rather quickly. I realize then that much of this life
here is fleeting. What seems important one day is soon
forgotten the next.

Bracelets with the initials *WWJD* (What Would Jesus Do?) have been popular in the past few years for that very reason; simplistically, they remind us to look at situations from Jesus' point of view, from His eternal perspective. It is impossible to do that and not soon after be convicted— thoroughly convinced that God would want you to share your wealth with those less fortunate. In this case, your spirit is winning the struggle.

I will not say it is that easy, or that after you have shared once, your spirit will forever rule the day. If it were that easy, we would not have the wars, violence, crime, and poverty throughout the world today, despite the fact we have entered the modern age and ought to know better.

Sharing your time can be more of a struggle. From the moment you are born, your days are finite, their exact number known only by God. And, there are literally only so many things you can do in a twenty-four hour day.

For me, it is a challenge to fit my life into a twenty-four hour block of days. Work, commuting, meals, sleep; this is the bulk of my work week. Then there are other obligations of being a member of a church and our society. And, of course, I want to spend as much time as I can with your Mother, and with each of you, not to mention Rex, Jelly-bean, or Gumdrop. Then comes my writing and the gardening. A forty-four hour day!

It is tough, but we must try nonetheless. We must be sensitive and attentive to requests or needs and do our best to help in any way we can.

Be a good listener, and you will find opportunities heading your way. You will adjust your schedule to fit it in.

God will bless you in ways you cannot imagine, in ways that might be different from what you would expect.

Always use your talents for the glory of God, not for your own glory. Everything given to you has been for a purpose—to serve God.

When you succeed, and you will, give all the praise to God. Nothing could have been accomplished had He not allowed it. He has given you the talent and the creative ideas and then mental capacity and tenacity to bring it all together.

If you put your talent in this perspective, you will quickly see that it all belongs to God. He doesn't want you to return it; He doesn't want you to keep it idle or hidden. On the contrary, He wants you to share it with those around you, particularly those who would benefit most.

Now, with regards to money, this should be the easiest of the three to share but, remarkably, it isn't always so. Again, though, if you consider that everything good flows from God, you will appreciate that it is God who gave you your talent, your good health, and the opportunity to earn an honest wage. You didn't do it alone. Don't let the worldly, self-centredness of your soul out-manoeuvre your quiet spirit, which instinctively knows that it all truly belongs to God.

God doesn't expect you to live in a cave or hut or live a monk's life. He wants you to experience the good life and to enjoy the fruits of your labour. At the same time, it is not right to feast in the park while a homeless man's stomach growls and churns.

Be generous all your days. Let your spirit be guided by the Holy Spirit so that others might also be blessed. Give in secret, though, so that you will truly know that it is the spirit which is guiding you and not your pride. If you do this, you will find yourself rewarded many times over, in ways you might not consider possible.

Remember, too, that a strengthened spirit is truly a blessing in and of itself.

Rich and poor have this in common:
The Lord is the Maker of them all
(Proverbs 22:2 NIV).

TIMOTHY RAY PHILLIPS

41 TEAL:

"Honour"

What is honour but being true to yourself, assuming that you are grounded in God's Word.

At Virginia Tech, where I went to school, one of my favourite places to go and think was above the War Memorial Chapel. It has a viewing area that overlooks the Drill Field. I would sit at the edge and watch all the students walking back and forth between the dorms and class.

I spent time there wondering how my life would turn out. Would I meet a girl soon? Would I get an A in calculus? Should I stay in Accounting or switch to English? Would I one day write the Great American novel? Would I travel and see the world? Would I marry and have children? Would my life make a difference?

Along this viewing area there are eight tall limestone pylons, each with a sculpted relief depicting a virtue: Brotherhood, Leadership, Sacrifice, Service, Loyalty, Duty, *Ut Prosim* ("That I may Serve"), and Honour.

Being among those sculpted men kept me in great company. Even on a snowy Friday night, my back against the cold Hokie stone, I never felt alone. Of course, I knew God was with me. But I was also surrounded by men in the act of doing great deeds.

Honour. There is no higher character trait. To be a person of conscience. One who knows right from wrong, and who strives to do what is right all the time. Even if the only one looking over his shoulder is God.

Temptation is all around us. The Devil sees to that. He wants nothing more than to lead God's children astray. He takes great delight when one of us stumbles and chooses the flesh over the spirit. He even thought he could tempt Jesus in the desert. For forty days he tried in vain. If he could spend forty days and nights on Jesus, who was perfect, how much more time will he spend on us who have a greater chance to succumb?

We do not have the spiritual strength of Jesus, but we do have His spirit dwelling in us. God, though, also gave us the gift of free will. We are not puppets or even Pinocchio's temporarily cut loose from the strings. We are boys and girls, first and foremost, with creative minds and wilful spirits. We do what we want, when we want, and no amount of reminding from your Earthly parents will change that. Not even the whispers of God can always keep us on the straight and narrow path.

It takes a keen ear to hear your inner voice—your conscience—when the pleasures of the flesh are calling. Powerful forces, they are. Pride, envy, gluttony, lust, anger, greed, and sloth. Pride is the worst of these Seven Deadly Sins, and you must guard against it all your life. It is in Man's nature to believe he can go it alone in the world. It is easy to believe that all you have accomplished in your life is the result of your own labours. We pray to God when we are low, when the storm clouds are swirling all around us. We fall to our knees at the thunder and plead for divine intervention. Then when the storm passes and the rainbows appear, we pat ourselves on the back for a 'job well done.'

That is Pride, and gradually, bit by bit, it chips away at our spiritual core. It is the Devil's way to lead us away from God. He takes advantage of our free will in his work against God. We are fallen men desperate to climb back on the pedestal no matter the cost. At that, the Devil is always willing to give a 'helping hand.'

The first step to fight pride—and a powerful adversary it is because you are fighting yourself—is to remind yourself that you are totally reliant on God's grace to survive and to thrive. That is called humility. Stay humble and hold fast to your honour.

It will be a hard battle because the more honourable you are, the more others will be attracted to you. They will put great stock in you and put you in positions of leadership. And when that happens, that alter-voice inside you will puff you up and try to convince you that all your success is your own doing. You will be prompted again and again to leave God in the dust, though it is He that pulled you out of the dust. Literally.

It will not be easy to be humble and successful at the same time. The latter will constantly tug at your humility. Failure is not the answer, though. Ask a homeless man or a drug addict or one in prison.

God has given you gifts and fruits of the spirit, and He wants you to use them wisely—not for your glory, but for

His. To build on His Kingdom to bring others out of the darkness and into the light.

Strive to be the best you can be, and when you are, take time to give thanks to God. When you do, He will bless you many times over.

Let Honour guide you in all you do. Stay true to God's Word and be a light to others around you. And, remember, in this spotlight you will be reflecting the grace of God. If that doesn't keep you humble, I don't know what will.

Like snow in summer and rain in harvest,
honour is not fitting for a fool
(Proverbs 26:1 NIV).

42 RED:
"Forgiveness"

Forgiveness is a tough word. Perhaps the toughest in the English language. All one million of them! Pride makes it so. I have mentioned that already. It is pride that makes us believe we can go it alone in the world. What rubbish that is. If God were to pull out from the world, it would take but a week for the Earth to come to a complete stop and leave half the world in perpetual darkness. And the other half sweltering in the heat!

It is pride that makes it so hard to forgive. Injured pride is a tough wound to heal. We pick at it continually, just when it is about healed. There is something to it that makes us loathe to give up the hurt. It is a weakness in our spirit.

God, through His Son, Jesus, forgives all of our sins. We are His children and there is nothing we can do that will keep us permanently at arm's-length from Him. We make a mistake, and we are forgiven.

That does not mean that our sins do not hurt God—or ourselves. Each wrong wounds our spirit and puts a distance between us and our Father in Heaven. God loves a contrite heart. We will always makes mistakes. Every day. That is part of being human in a fallen world; it is a by-product of having a free will. How we respond and correct those mistakes are what is important.

You will learn this when you are older and have children of your own. Being a parent in itself puts you a step closer in God's shoes. Children are, by nature, immature. Selfish at first and wanting every physical need fulfilled. Immediately. Now!

Raising children is not risk-free. Wonderful moments abound, but so do hurts and disappointment. Realizing your child has a mind of his or her own is a shock in itself. But there is nothing a child can do—nothing you can do—that will diminish a parent's love for him. Or for her.

So it is with God. For all of us. We are His children for all times. We sin; we err. We ask to be forgiven, and He responds with a loud YES!

It is amazing, then, how hard it is for us to forgive others. After all, we have a perfect model, a constant model. Throughout the Bible we see Jesus teaching about forgiveness. And He knew—He knows—how hard it is for us to follow His example.

Remember the parable in the Bible about the Unforgiving Debtor in Matthew 18:23? A king forgave a large debt from a servant because that man got on his knees and pleaded for mercy and time to repay. Granted his wish, the man left and demanded payment of a much smaller amount from a fellow servant. This indebted servant also fell to his knees and asked for time and mercy, but the first servant—even though he had experienced forgiveness first-hand—refused and threw the man and his family into jail.

Remember the outcome? When the king found out what had happened, he had the first servant thrown into prison until he could repay every penny. The king was angry that the servant did not pass on a little of the mercy he had received from the king.

When the disciple Peter asks Jesus how many times he should forgive a person, Jesus replies 'Seventy times seven.' Seven, of course, is the number of perfection, of God, of infinity.

Just as God will forgive us countless times, even for the same sin, so should we forgive others.

Not an easy task, of course. After all, we are human and far from perfect. That silly pride keeps getting in the way. We see others' sins far more clearly than our own. We put ourselves in the place of God. That is what pride does. And it is this pride that keeps us from being able to forgive.

If you hold on to a hurt, trust me, you will never move forward. The hurt will keep you in the past. Real growth comes in the present and prepares you for the future. There are lessons to be learned from the past, but little to be gained from dwelling in it. On this, you must trust me, and what is written in the Bible.

Forgive as the Lord forgave you
(Colossians 3:13 NIV).

TIMOTHY RAY PHILLIPS

43 SCARLET:

"God's Love"

On the surface, convincing someone of God's love is as difficult as describing faith. If you cannot "see" God, how do you know He exists? A dead man can't exhale.

But I look at it this way. If I go outside at night and the sky is pitch black, is it true to say it means the sun no longer shines? I cannot see its rays or feel its warm heat, so it must have been extinguished at day's end. Yet we all know from Kindergarten, if not before, the Earth spins and moves around the sun. The sun never stops shining but at any given time half the planet is on the far side looking away from the sun.

Of course, it helps to have a situation so precise you can set your clock to it. We wake up with the sun in our eyes and are reaffirmed that the sun does exist. The newspapers can even tell you the exact moment the sun will rise in three months' time. We are smart in our thinking to know that the sun shines continuously even during our nights.

It is admittedly more difficult to accept by faith that God exists and then to take the next step and realize that

God loves us. So much so that He came down to Earth in the form of a man—which were created in His image—to live among us, teach us, admonish us, work with us and, most of all, love us. He took the hardest step of all. He walked into the lion's den of hate and ignorance knowing full-well what lay ahead. He knew the future and yet still took up the cross for us. As Jesus Himself says in the Bible, there is no greater love than that a man should lay down his life for a friend.

As Jesus, God made the supreme sacrifice for us, and to consider that the Creator of all things would do that for me, and for you, is more than humbling. The words "God loves you" seem trite because they are sometimes used in a tone or time that seriously underemphasize the great sacrifice of Jesus on the cross, but the words are true and powerful. God does love us.

God suffered much on the cross so that the sins that naturally separate us from the Creator, could be removed forever. Why did God do this? Quite simply, so that we would never be apart from Him. He has prepared a great house for us in Heaven, and one day we will all be living there together. And those moments of hard choices will seem like a far-away memory. The pains of this world will no longer be measured or remembered.

This is our future and it is guaranteed to you because you have accepted Christ as your personal Saviour. The Bible is clear: *If you confess with your mouth that "Jesus is Lord" and believe in your heart that He rose from the dead, you will be saved (Romans 10:9 NIV).* You will have an eternal seat at the Lord's table.

God is not content to wait until the end times to be an active part of our lives, just as your Mother and I do not wait in the distance until you reach adulthood before we are a constant part of your lives. You need us in order to grow to proper maturity—emotionally, and especially spiritually. Love is the power that brings out that growth. You need the security, warmth, attention, guidance and love of your parents. You need the same from God.

The incredible fact in this is God's strong desire to be active in all our lives. There are over seven billion souls in this world, and God wants nothing more than to be able to bring them all into his house. He is a God of incredible, unending love.

To God, the age and heat of the sun is no more than the flicker of a firefly. A thousand years is but a nano-second to Him, and the brilliance of the sun little more than an ember from a dying fire.

I read once that if our sun were the dot of an 'i' on this page, the next closest sun would be ten miles away. And there are billions of suns in the universe, all created by one God, a god who, despite all His power and all His knowledge, took the time to walk among us as a man two thousand years ago. For those who have claimed Him, He lives within each of them today. My dear children, God's love is inside you, even as you read these words. It is the source of your beating heart. His spirit within you has been melded with your soul and made you a child of God. A child of the Creator of the Universe. How awesome is that?

Like all good parents, God loves His children with all His heart. Feel blessed that He has called you His own.

The Lord's unfailing love surrounds
the man who trusts in him
(Psalm 32:10 NIV).

44 EBONY:

"Grace"

Grace. It is a simple word with a pleasing sound, but it is the most powerful word in our language. It is God's love for us, a love so intense and complete that it removes any distance that could exist between us lowly mortals and the Creator of the Universe.

It is by God's grace that our souls are freed from the mortal bondage of our bodies; by His grace, at our earthly death, we will rise into His presence and live forever in a complete and undiminished joy.

When you accepted Christ, you opened your heart and allowed His spirit to enter and breathe a new life to your soul. God's grace forever changed your soul into a spiritual being with an eternal life. His grace lives in you and is called upon by you in times of concern, distress, loneliness, confusion, or temptation.

Grace is mercy. Permanent relief, or pardon, for our many sins, both the significant and the petty. Grace is given to the offender by the very one he has offended. We are clay creatures who fell out of grace almost as soon as we stood up. Life was simple in the Garden of Eden, and God's laws were simple: eat from any tree but the Tree of Knowledge of Good and Evil.

The story is familiar to you, I know. The Devil, disguised as a serpent, appealed to man's ego to be in control of his own destiny, to be self-sufficient, god-like. So he manipulated our free will and we ate from the very Tree of Knowledge. The innocence of coming directly from God's hand was instantly gone, and sin became part of our collective DNA, which remains with us today. Satan was successful that day in separating us from our Maker.

Fortunately, the story—our story—doesn't end with our banishment from the Garden with the Tree of Life. God's plan is that we would always be with Him. By His grace, He sent His Son Jesus, fully divine and fully man, to walk among us. He preached the Good News that God's loves us despite our mortal flaws. Jesus, the living tree of life, gave up His life for us on the cross. Through His death, the cross became our tree of life.

Grace is important to each of us in three ways. First, if we believe in Him, our presence in Heaven is secure. Second, accepting His grace takes the pressure off of us. We do not need to measure up to a divine yardstick that is beyond our reach. God knows first-hand what it is like to live as a mortal in a fallen world. Perfection is unattainable for us, and that is ok. We are loved for who we are. That is not a free ticket to commit sin, but it is a relief from the pressure to be perfect.

Third, we are called to mirror God's grace on our fellow brethren. Do not be man who, though he received relief from the king for debts he owed, refused to give similar relief to someone who owed him only one percent as much. We know the outcome. When the king discovered what the man had done, the monarch had the man thrown into jail—the same thing that ungrateful man had done to the servant who had asked for relief.

It is not well or wise to relish in God's grace and withhold our own from others. Be gracious in your relationships with others. Try to see their life from their shoes; be lenient when you can. Turn the other cheek. Lend a hand. Keep them in your daily prayers. If they are a believer, pray that they would show grace to others; if they do not yet believe, pray that God would touch their hearts so they would openly receive His grace.

Keep your ears open to God's whispers, and follow his lead.

As for you, you were dead in your transgressions and sins, in which you used to live when you followed the ways of the world...Like the rest, we were by nature objects of wrath. But because of his great love for us, God, who is rich in mercy, made us alive with Christ even when we were dead in transgressions—it is by grace you have been saved. And God raised us up with Christ and seated us with him in the heavenly realms (Ephesians 2:1-6; NIV).

TIMOTHY RAY PHILLIPS

45 CANARY:

"Hope"

When I think of hope, I think first of a canary. Continually singing even while in the dark depths of a mine. That continual singing that told the miners there was still enough oxygen left to breathe. Great hopes—life and death—rested between the wings of the tiny bird.

Nowadays the mines have sophisticated equipment to gauge the air quality. The canary has been retired to his cage by the living-room window.

Hope locked in a cage.

On the surface, that seems ironic. Hope should be the epitome of freedom; it should be more like the eagle soaring in the high winds. Not the picture of a yellow bird singing and swaying inside a domed caged.

Hope is the antithesis of hell. The possibility of positive change, the antecedent of Real.

But dreams don't 'just happen.' Remember Dorothy in *The Wizard of Oz*? She could have clicked her ruby red slippers three times in *Munchkinland* and gone straightaway home. Of course, she would have missed an incredible adventure along the way (not to mention making three great new friends), and Frank Baum's classic would have been reduced to a ten-page short story. More importantly, Dorothy—and the reader—would have learned nothing along the way. She instead put her hope in a wizard she had never met.

If you have no hope in life, you have no life. It's that simple. Hope unreached—unfulfilled—is only half a life. It is a waste of life.

So if the canary is Hope, what is the cage? The obvious answer is any obstacle that keeps your hopes from becoming reality. But I wonder, how much of the cage is self-imposed? Do we keep the canary in permanent exile for fear of actually succeeding? What if the Reality is a disappointment in comparison to the Dream? What if the original hope was too much of a stretch in the first place—an intentional, convenient placeholder to having a real plan?

We fool ourselves every day with artificial hope. It is a great excuse for putting hard work off to another day.

Hope is not a static thing; it is not a stuffed toy. The canary in the cage is really alive. She eats, drinks, sleeps, and moves. And, yes, she even poops. Some dreams will fizzle; some will even sizzle before they fizzle, which is even more disheartening when they eventually fall apart.

As a writer, I have felt the edge of the stage a number of times; I could even imagine the warm flush of the limelight but, then, nothing. Life is like that. Just when you are on the verge of a breakthrough, you are back to Square One. Read any biography of Thomas Edison if you want to understand both reality and persistence intertwined.

Remember, though, that hope does more than just move you forward. It leads you, uncontrollably at times, to sing. Even a new song from time to time. As you can imagine, though, a song sung in a cage—gilded though it may be—will have but a fraction of the joy that it would have on the outside.

Open the cage and let the canary rest in your two hands. If it poops, so be it. Don't be afraid to let it fly. Just keep your eyes on the bright colour and do your best to keep up.

If you're lucky, you'll find yourself singing along the way.

Find rest, O my soul, in God alone;
my hope comes from him
(Psalm 62:5 NIV).

46 TURQUOISE BLUE:
"Peace"

At night we sleep and in those few hours we are all the same. The famous and the infamous; the plain and the fancy. It is a level playing field then. In those dark hours we are all vulnerable to nightmares, thieves who enter the house, and the chance, however slim, that we will never wake up again on this Earth.

I find some comfort in the fact that even the most powerful people on Earth must at some point close their eyes and take a rest. It reminds us all that we are mortal. We are not in control after all. If we were, we would not need to rest. Our bodies would not show the tell-tale signs of aging.

God does not rest, and He is ageless.

When are you most at peace? When you are awake or asleep? Unless your sub-conscious is overactive in the nightmare department, it is when you are at rest. Your body gives up trying to control everything around it, and instead focuses inward on re-charging and refreshing.

The downfall to peace is worry. What will other people think? How will I pay for it? What if I'm not accepted in the group? What if someone finds out about my dirty little secret? What if I never get married? What if I make a bad choice? What if I'm never happy? What if I disappoint my parents? What if I disappoint myself? What if I wake up near the end of my life and think it was all a waste?

Worry stirs up the emotional well which, for most people, runs quite deep and is inky dark. We add to it constantly for fear it would run dry, and then what would we do? Be truly happy? How unrealistic is that!

Some days I wish I could read the minds of the other animals—the ones on four legs or two wings. Do they worry the way we humans do? I doubt they worry about their looks or whether they have enough friends. Their main concern is to eat and to not be eaten. Pretty simple, and if they can sun themselves in a meadow some afternoon or play in the water a while, so much the better. But I doubt they worry over the endless possibilities each new day brings.

Now, you can say that they are only animals and have not been blessed with higher brain power like ourselves. They have a limited capacity to imagine. That may be true, but with our higher brain function comes the ability to reason and to talk through our problems with others. We have the opportunities to work through our problems and prevent everyone from rushing over an emotional cliff like lemmings.

For all our possibilities, we mortals are a worry-centric creature. It got so bad that God Himself had to come down and show us the way and, even then, two thousand years later we are still not at peace. With ourselves, our family, neighbours or other nations.

The crux seems to be our self-esteem. Often, we don't love ourselves enough or, for some, we love it too much. Finding the healthy balance seems to be an elusive possibility for most, most likely because of a rocky upbringing. As in most aspects of our character, self-esteem is shaped, fired, and glazed early on. If an individual is deeply broken, the problem very likely originated before they were an adult.

I have read it in many places so I believe it to be true: all wars are at their source based on economics. Generally one people wanting something another group has. It is about land, resources, and people. It is only later that a moral stamp of imprimatur is added to make it a cause.

Take the American Civil War. Today we learn in school and believe it was a *morally-inspired* war primarily to end slavery, with the North opposing slavery and the South supporting it. But that is not the whole story. While there were strong passions in the background surrounding slavery, the core issue was states' rights and economics.

The industrialized North was growing richer than the rural South with each passing year. It wasn't until after bloody Antietam in September 1862 that Lincoln had the political courage to move forward with his Emancipation Proclamation and even then the impact was limited in scope. From the North's view, their primary goal in the early years of the war was to preserve the Union, which meant a preservation of the status quo—one that included slavery. In my opinion, the greatest blight on our nation's history.

I remember my high school history teacher saying that economics was at the core of every war. It goes back to the sand box and Tommy has the toy that Timmy wants to have. A battle royal ensues, with flying sand and forceful fists. The origin of the fight is envy, which triggers hatred.

War is simply the sandbox times a trillion. The origin and the objectives are the same. Domination over another for economic gain. Which is expected to bring a more pleasurable and more secure life.

Some would also argue that the American Revolution was about life, liberty, and the pursuit of happiness. That would possibly be true if you substituted happiness for wealth. At its infancy, the rebellion was economic-based (No Taxation without Representation).

The same case could be made about World War II: Japan's unquenchable thirst for natural resources on the Asian continent; Adolph Hitler's rise out of hyperinflationary Germany.

I could list example after example. There have been wars since the beginning. The first recorded murder was Cain killing his brother Abel. Why did he do it? He was jealous because his brother's gift was more pleasing to God than his own. Jealousy and self-esteem came into play, as does economics. He wanted to receive God's blessing and that of his father, Adam.

History repeated itself somewhat with the twin sons of the Biblical Isaac. Esau was the older of the twins and Isaac's favourite and would inherit his father's blessing and possessions. It was his birth-right as the eldest. Twin Jacob wanted Esau's birth-right and in a moment of weakness for Esau, the older sold it to Jacob for a simple bowl of stew. Esau quickly regretted his decision and despised his brother. This trickery led to a hatred between Esau and Jacob, and Jacob feared for his life.

But as the Bible records throughout, this desire for earthly riches is all folly. At some point, within a century of being born, a person will die, and any earthly possessions will remain behind. While we have history books, the vast majority of the over <u>one hundred billion plus</u> souls who have lived on Earth are now unknown to the modern civilized world. Their contributions are now anonymous. Any comforts they had enjoyed are now long gone—destroyed or being used by a total stranger.

So why do we care so much about what we have on Earth? Why do we worry about being a star or the most liked? Clearly, the only thing that matters is what lies on the other side. Jesus came to Earth to give us hope and a glimpse of the eternal Heaven. He came as the Prince of Peace, to rid the Earth of its wars and the ugliness that happens in the process and that follows in its wake.

Each of us is on a journey. For those of us who have accepted Christ as our Saviour, we know the ending. From acceptance until our earthly death we are on a course known only to God. Like any parent, He wants only the best for His children. He wants us to be happy and at peace—with ourselves and those around us.

If it is possible, as far as it depends on you, live at peace with everyone (Romans 12:18 NIV).

I truly believe that our ability to be at real peace depends on:

- ❖ How well we love ourselves (our self-esteem);
- ❖ How satisfied we are with our life (happy kids don't start fights);
- ❖ Our eternal perspective (God is in control; Heaven is worth the wait).

Each of us, at some point, will close our eyes and wake up on the other side. When that happens, we will have the full knowledge that now eludes us. We will then understand how so much of life here is made petty. That will be a watershed moment for us.

We know enough from the Bible, though, to understand that there is God's plan and the Devil's plan. Good vs. Evil. God is peace and joy and love. The Devil is war, discontent, and hate. Worry is the Devil's workshop.

One of the most comforting verses in Scripture is Matthew 6:33-34: *But seek first his kingdom and his righteousness and all these things will be given to you as well. Therefore do not worry about tomorrow, for tomorrow will worry about itself. Each day enough trouble of its own (NIV).* We need to put our full trust in God.

Seek peace in everything you do. Seek God's guidance through prayer, and focus on the Heaven above you, not the worries in front of you. If you do this, you will, in the Apostle Paul's words, be running the good race and fighting the Good fight.

May the God of hope fill you with all joy and peace
as you trust in him, so that you may overflow with hope
by the power of the Holy Spirit
(Romans 15:13 NIV).

47 Wisteria:

"Nostalgia"

It is natural and, I suppose, extremely human to look back at our past from time to time. Such views are a part of our creative mind, a unique gift from God. I doubt, for example, that giraffes think about their days on the savannah the previous summer. Or that rabbits lounge lazily in their burrow relishing the radishes of their yesteryears. Sure, they say elephants never forget, but do they dream wistfully, nostalgically, of their kinder days?

Man alone has this particular gift to connect the dots and put past events together in their memory cells and then be moved by them. We do this daily. Partly to escape the pain or the pressures of this day. We add a happy filter to our memories so that the old days almost always play back as the good old days.

Is this a defence mechanism to protect us from past hurts or it is a reflection of our growing maturity? Are we re-writing history or putting it in its proper perspective now that we have grown up a bit more?

There are people—you know them—who let the past run their lives. They had one bad experience or embarrassing moment or made one mistake, and it haunts them. They let it not just run their lives, but ruin it in the process. They have forgotten that God forgives all sins if you ask Him. The God of the universe forgives freely; the god of our Soul does not.

We are competing daily for the supremacy of our Soul. God desires it. Our Self wants it. The Evil One covets it. For us, it springs from our desire, ever since we could first think, to be our own person, to feel that we are in charge of our own destiny.

This streak of independence is particularly deep in the American people, so it is Godly-inspired that there are so many Evangelicals in this country. Sadly, though, it is not a universal phenomenon throughout the nation. Nor do all Believers reminisce with the proper perspective. For them, nostalgia is not a chance to remember God's grace and goodness for saving us or for giving us a moment of joy and fun. Nor is it an opportunity to realize how much we have grown, or appreciate how far we have come.

If you are serious about being a follower of Christ, you must pack up all the bad past moments of your life and leave the baggage at the side of the road before you take another step in the road. This is, by the way, a daily discipline. Leave your sins and the memory of them behind you, just as you would tell Satan to get behind you.

And you must tell him that out loud, you know, because he, unlike God, cannot read your mind. He is clever enough and experienced over the centuries to read our faces and understand human nature, but it is truly impossible for him to read your mind. Your inner thoughts can only be touched by God and you. Some thoughts, the ancient memories, are hidden even to you. God, though, is omniscient. He knows us. He is the God of wisteria and all the other colours of the universe.

From the moment of our birth we are on a journey. Each day is a day spent, a move closer to the other side of our mortality. In between are billions of experiences—good, bad, and ugly. They occur throughout our days with little forethought and much afterthought. Hence, the old expression, "Look before you leap." But that is not in the general nature of man. Even as adults, we are too much like children. It is a long road to spiritual maturity, the true goal of every Believer.

My advice to you is simple. Enjoy the days God has given you. Make the most of them, and reflect on them from time to time. Appreciate your progress, and stay the course. Most important, learn from your past but do not dwell on it. Be right with God and those you may have hurt, and then turn the page to a new day.

Forget the former things;
do not dwell on the past
(Isaiah 43:18 NIV).

48 GOLD:

"Heaven"

In Ecclesiastes 3:19-20 the Bible says *that Man's fate is like that of the animals; the same fate awaits them both: As one dies, so dies the other. All have the same breath; man has no advantage over the animal. Everything is meaningless. All go to the same place; all come from dust, and to dust all shall return (NIV).*

This is an intriguing passage. We know from Genesis that God made man out of the dust and to dust we shall return. He also breathed the "breath of life" into Adam, and this unique spirit combined with our body to give us our soul, our unique personality.

Were it not for the spirit within us, we would perish completely at the moment our heart stopped. But Ecclesiastes goes on to say in 3:21: *"Who knows if the spirit of man rises upward and if the spirit of the animal goes down into the earth? (NIV).*

These are words from the Old Testament, before Christ became man and walked among us. This is before His sacrifice on the cross and resurrection into Heaven. The answer to King Solomon's question is hinted earlier in verse 3:11: *He has also set eternity in the hearts of men; yet they cannot fathom what God has done from beginning to end (NIV).*

But how has he set eternity in our hearts? The answer is given in the New Testament. We are saved for eternity by the grace of God (not by our own efforts): *This grace was given us in Christ Jesus before the beginning of time, but it has now been revealed through the appearing of our Saviour, Christ Jesus, who has destroyed death and has brought life and immortality to light through the gospel"* (2 Timothy 1: 9-10 NIV).

God's divinity and supremacy is clear. He existed before the beginning. That is a hard concept, even for a middle-aged adult, but we accept it by faith.

Not only did God exist before anything else existed, He had already decided before we even existed that we would live forever in His presence. He knew that Man would fall; he understood the weakness of the human spirit compared to the (free) wilfulness of man's soul. And He understood the evil of the Devil.

Yet, although He knew we would fall before Adam had taken his first breath, He already had a plan in motion that would involve the sacrifice of His Son thousands of years later.

We were destined to live with our Creator in His home in Heaven.

He has made everything beautiful in its time.
He has also set eternity in the hearts of men;
yet they cannot fathom what God
has done from beginning to end
(Ecclesiastes 3:11 NIV).

IN LOVING COLOUR

Imperatives & Attributes of the Soul

A Father's Imperative.......... iii

Adventure 81

Beginnings............................9

Character 85

Compassion 169

Competition 93

Courage............................. 117

Disappointment.................. 107

Divine Imperative i

Education............................31

Envy....................................97

Faith 125

First Love............................51

Forgiveness........................ 183

Foundations 21

Friendship 47

Generosity.......................... 173

God's Love 187

Grace................................. 191

Happiness............................75

Hard Choices........................67

Hard Work 89

Health 63

Heaven............................... 209

Honour............................... 179

Hope 195

Imagination......................... 39

In a Blink.............................. v

Inside the Box........................ 7

Kindness 161

Loss................................... 111

Loyalty 43

Memories 131

Music & Laughter............... 59

Nostalgia............................ 205

Passion............................... 139

Peace 199

Perspective.......................... 13

Poetry................................ 153

Prayer 121

Purity 55

Reflection........................... 135

Resolution.......................... 101

Respect 157

Self-Sacrifice........................ 71

Solitude.............................. 147

Stewardship 143

Tenderness............................35

Tithing 149

Uniqueness 27

Visions & Goals....................17

ABOUT THE AUTHOR

Timothy Ray Phillips grew up in the Amish country of Lancaster County, Pennsylvania. Here he found his poetic heart and began writing poetry at the age of thirteen. The small Moravian town of Lititz was a perfect backdrop for Timothy's earliest poems. Much of his work reflects his experience and affinity for small town America.

At seventeen Timothy moved south to attend college at Virginia Polytechnic Institute in Blacksburg, Virginia. He graduated *cum laude* with a Bachelor's degree in Accounting. He earned his Master's degree in Business Administration from Azusa Pacific University in California. He is both a Certified Public Accountant (CPA) and a Certified Internal Auditor (CIA). Currently, he is the Chief Financial Officer for a privately-held company in Blacksburg. He jokes that he balances numbers by day and words by night. Timothy is an admitted night owl and it is in the small hours that his most creative work surfaces.

In Loving Colour is Timothy's first published book of prose. He is currently finishing his second book of fiction, which he hopes to publish later this year.

Timothy, his wife Debbie, and their three children (the impetus and inspiration for this book) live in beautiful Ellett Valley just east of Blacksburg. Their beached ark includes two lemon-white beagles, a Maltese, two parakeets and, at last count, twenty-three wild deer. Not to mention a treasure trove of musically-inclined birds.

www.ingramcontent.com/pod-product-compliance
Lightning Source LLC
Chambersburg PA
CBHW070802280326
41934CB00012B/3020